STO

12·6·79

A Doctor's Life

Nicholas S. Assali

A DOCTOR'S LIFE

Harcourt Brace Jovanovich

New York and London

*Requests for permission to make copies of
any part of the work should be mailed to:
Permissions, Harcourt Brace Jovanovich, Inc.
757 Third Avenue, New York, N.Y. 10017*

Printed in the United States of America

Library of Congress Cataloging in Publication Data

*Assali, Nicholas S.
A doctor's life.*

Includes index.
1. *Assali, Nicholas S.* 2. *Gynecologists—United States—Biography.*
3. *Obstetricians—United States—Biography.*
4. *Gynecologists—Brazil—Biography.*
5. *Obstetricians—Brazil—Biography.*
I. *Title.*
RG76.A84A33   618'.092'4 [B]   79–1808
ISBN 0–15–126161–X

First edition

B C D E

Contents

C877454

PART THREE
The United States

PART FOUR
California

*I wish to acknowledge the invaluable help
given me in writing this book by
my editor, Drenka Willen.*

A Doctor's Life is a portrait of a man of
great professional accomplishment,
great courage, and great compassion in
the face of terrific odds.

Nicholas Assali is Professor of Obstet-
rics and Gynecology and Chief of the Di-
vision of Reproductive Physiology at the
University of California, Los Angeles,
and founder and former president of the
Society for Gynecologic Investigation.
In 1978 he received the Virginia Apgar
Award in Perinatal Pediatrics from the
American Academy of Pediatrics for out-
standing research in perinatalogy.
He lives in Pacific Palisades, California,
with his wife, Pauline, and his two sons,
Robin and Billy.

Presumptuous Man! The reason wouldst Thou find,
Why formed so weak, so little, and so blind?
First, if Thou canst, the harder reason guess,
Why formed no weaker, blinder and no less?

. . . .

So Man, who here seems principal alone,
Perhaps acts second to some sphere unknown,
Touches some wheel, or verges to some goal;
'Tis but a part we see, and not a whole.

ALEXANDER POPE

From "An Essay On Man"
Epistle I

Part One

LEBÁNON

1 · Death in the Desert

IN the early morning of a beautiful spring day in 1925, the French captain in command of the Senegalese troops surrounding the town of Rachaya ordered his artillery to open fire. As I learned several years later, the captain commanded his troops to concentrate on the massive fortress, called the Elkaala, which dominated the town. But the men of the Senegalese artillery, who were notorious for their savagery, apparently disregarded the order. The shells exploded everywhere—in the mud huts of the poor, in the stone and brick homes of the rich, in stores, corrals, and barns. The result was systematic destruction of the town. Each explosion scattered fragments of human bodies, along with those of horses, donkeys, sheep, and goats.

Those of us, mostly children and women, who had taken refuge in the basement of the Catholic church could feel the earth and the massive walls of the church tremble with each explosion, as if shaken by an earthquake. The fear that any minute one of those shells would hit the church and bring its roof and walls down on our heads left us numb. The smaller children screamed and cried; the older ones kept asking their mothers when all of this would end. I repeated that question to my mother a hundred times. "Why doesn't Jesus help us, if we're hiding in his home? Why does God allow this?" My mother answered, "It will be over soon, soon. Don't be afraid! God will protect this church and save us. Your father will be here any time now to rescue us." But the shells continued to explode for the next two hours. A short silence, then sudden cacophony. The rattling of machine guns and rifles was getting closer to the outskirts of the town. Fear had by now all but paralyzed us. We children were terrified by the thought that the savage black soldiers were already inside the church and might discover our hiding place. Many of us were convinced that we would never leave the basement alive. Yet my mother kept her composure. She went from one child to another, patting, reassuring, handing out cookies, raisins, goat cheese, and bread.

The tide of terror continued to sweep the town; the firing and grenade explosions went on unabated. The commander of the Senegalese troops had ordered his infantry to advance and seize the Elkaala, where the revolutionary forces were quartered. "Nothing must stop you," he told his soldiers. "Burn and destroy anything that gets in your way. The Elkaala has to be taken and its occupants annihilated!"

The Lebanese revolutionary force firing on the French mercenaries from the Elkaala numbered about two hundred. These gallant men had defeated the French garrison of Rachaya only forty-eight hours before. My father, Salem, was their leader. He had been organizing the revolution against French colonialism for two or three years. He had planned to storm the French garrison in the Elkaala, take the fortress, and hold the French soldiers hostage. The revolutionaries counted on the help of other towns and cities, which had promised to revolt and overthrow the arrogant French masters who considered the Lebanese and Syrians "dirty animals." My father and his followers had had their property and crops confiscated by the French authorities without any explanation or compensation. Salem's young sister had been killed by a French soldier while nursing her newborn baby; the assassin had been released shortly afterward for "insufficient evidence."

So when my father and his companions decided to revolt, they had high hopes that French rule in Lebanon and Syria would be terminated by force or by negotiation from a strong position. They had taken their simple weapons from French headquarters or bought them on the black market. The ammunition was hidden in places known only to the leader and a few trusted aides.

On the appointed day, the revolutionaries met in the mountains about ten miles from Rachaya. Arms were distributed. Disguised as Lebanese policemen, some of the men entered the Elkaala and infiltrated the French garrison. The rest crept through the darkness and surrounded the fortress. A rifle shot was heard, and then firing started simultaneously inside and out. In less than three hours the French garrison was overwhelmed and the fortress was occupied by the victorious revolutionary force.

Alas, the victory of the revolution was short-lived. Support from other towns and cities did not come in time to prevent French reinforcements from arriving. The uprisings expected in other Lebanese and Syrian areas did not materialize. The French army headquarters, located some twenty miles from Rachaya, promptly dispatched about 2,000 well-trained and battle-seasoned Senegalese mercenaries. This unit was equipped with modern armaments. They were known for their ruthlessness, and their appearance terrorized the population.

The French reinforcements slowly encircled the town. Only the road to Mount Hermon was still open. The destruction of the town and the annihilation of all resistance was ordered and meticulously executed.

A week before the outbreak of the Lebanese revolution, my father had prepared the family for the events to come. He had gathered my mother, his mother, and his children around him and alerted them to the hard days ahead. He explained that the struggle was a choice between living with honor and liberty or continuing to grovel as slaves. The family accepted his message without dissent. My mother began to stock food, clothing, and other essentials in baskets and boxes.

On the evening before the storming of the Elkaala, my father moved the family to the basement of the Catholic church two blocks away. He knew that our home, made of mud and timbers, was too weak to withstand vibrations; also, it was suspect and apt to be searched by the enemy. The church, on the other hand, was built much more solidly, of stones and tiles, and, owing to religious tradition, the French soldiers would not search it. Despite all these precautions, Salem was certain that the revolution would not last too long and that he would soon return to the family a victorious leader who had defeated French colonialism.

His dreams, however, were short-lived. After the bombardment, the Senegalese infantry advanced toward the town, firing machine guns and rifles, throwing hand grenades aimlessly, burning every structure and massacring every living creature in their way. They finally reached the center of the town and saw nothing to stop them except the massive, towering fortress. It was still there, seemingly intact despite all the shelling. The defenders of the Elkaala were firing from the roofs, windows, and doors, inflicting heavy casualties. The dumbfounded French commander lost his composure. He shouted to his troops, "Storm the damned thing! Burn down everything around it! Crush every stone and window! Gun down every man inside!" Yet every time the Senegalese troops attempted a direct assault, they were met by a hail of bullets.

The frustrated commander finally concentrated all his large guns on the fortress and ordered a continuous bombardment. The battle for the Elkaala lasted about eighteen hours. During that time the ammunition of the revolutionary force became nearly exhausted, and the firing from the fortress slackened. The Senegalese renewed their assault with greater fury. Backed by heavy shelling and concentrated machine-gun fire, they stormed the entrance.

My father realized that further resistance was not possible. He told his men that the situation was hopeless and that the revolution had failed. "Everyone must try to escape from the fortress and save himself!" he shouted. "The road to the mountains is still open, but everyone is free to find his own route of escape!" After saying good-bye to some of his dearest friends, he and a few others jumped through a window down into one of the ravines surrounding the Elkaala. When he reached the ground, a bullet hit him in the side. He managed to drag himself into some bushes, and he hid there until most of the Senegalese troops had entered the fortress.

Though he was in pain, bleeding profusely, and growing weaker, he was determined to reach the church and tell his family what to do. He tore his shirt to bandage his wound. Leaning on his rifle, he limped slowly through the darkness to the basement of the Catholic church.

Those men who were unable to escape from the Elkaala were immediately captured by the Senegalese and disarmed. They were ordered to line up in a double row in the courtyard. When all of them were facing the bayonets and the machine guns of the Senegalese, the French commander approached them. He was followed by about a dozen soldiers, each carrying a loaded revolver. He put his revolver against the first revolutionary's head and fired. The man fell dead. The French officer did the same with each of the other men, stopping only to load the revolver when it was empty. When he was finished, 180 bodies were lying on the ground. No questions were asked, no answers given.

Sweating, pale, and bleeding, my father reached the church and burst into its basement. He fell into the arms of his wife and his mother. He told the crowd what had happened. Some women began crying hysterically and asking what had happened to their husbands. The church basement became a bedlam of terror-stricken women and children, screaming and even fighting with each other.

My father drank some water, but was unable to eat. My mother tore off a piece of bedsheet and wrapped it tightly around his wound. He gathered the little energy left him and told us to follow. Each of us carried as much food and provisions as he could. My mother took a bedsheet so that she could change my father's dressing after it became soaked with blood.

Still using his rifle as a crutch and leaning on my mother, my father and his family left the church basement that night and followed the deserted road to the slope of Mount Hermon. He knew this road well; in his youth he had used it many times as a fugitive from the Turkish army. When we reached the outskirts of the town, we looked behind us and saw devastation. Rachaya was in flames, and the smoke carried the smell of burning human and animal flesh. We heard at a distance the screams of men, women, and children, as well as the sounds of animals running wild among the burning houses. Tears poured from our eyes. We realized that we had lost not only our house, farm, and herds, but also many of our friends and all hope of living in freedom.

My father led the family along the deserted road. With each minute that passed he lost more blood and grew weaker. Finally, about five miles from the town and despite all our help, he told us to stop because his end was near. He lay on the ground and asked us to stand in a circle around him. He talked to the five terrified young boys and one girl, to my mother and his mother.

"I tried to give freedom and dignity to my fellow men, and to liberate my country so that my own children and those of others could be free. Not only have I totally failed, but also I have brought pain, agony, and misery upon you and others. From now on, you will know nothing but humiliation, poverty, and indignity." Then he looked straight into the eyes of my older brother, Issa, and into my eyes, and asked us to take care of the rest of the family. He went on: "Whatever adversity you may encounter in the future, don't fear to fight for what you think is right. Don't be afraid to tell the truth, whatever the consequences. Be compassionate to your fellow men, even if sometimes you'd rather admire a dog than a man!"

As he pronounced these last words, he lapsed into unconsciousness and shortly thereafter died. We gathered around his body in the middle of the night, weeping silently; only the moon and the stars provided a glimmer of light. Although we were all stunned by the magnitude of the tragedy, my mother regained her composure rapidly and told the children that they could not leave the body of their dead father exposed to wild animals on the deserted road. "We have to bury him, no matter what," she said. But the children had nothing to dig a grave with. The boys were told to start clearing an area adjacent to the road with their own hands and sharp pieces of rock. The women gathered stones, branches, and whatever else they could find to cover the dead body. Finally we managed to dig a shallow grave with our bare hands, then we lifted my father's body and placed it in the ground.

We had barely begun covering the body with stones and branches when suddenly we heard shouts: "Halt! Raise your arms!" We found ourselves facing members of a Senegalese patrol who had tracked my father down. We were terrified.

The patrol sergeant approached my mother and asked, "Where is your husband?" She pointed to the body partially covered with stones. "So you're trying to hide him?"

"He's dead. He was hit by a bullet. He lost a lot of blood and died."

"You're lying." He hit my mother with the butt of his rifle. My brother and I rushed toward him in an effort to protect her, but we were stopped by the other Senegalese soldiers and beaten badly. I received a cut over my left eye. The scar remains to this day and is a continuing reminder of those terrifying moments. The soldiers were ordered to uncover my father's body.

"Be sure he's dead for good," said the sergeant. "Bayonet him straight to the heart."

Two of the soldiers advanced toward my father's body, unsheathed their bayonets, and plunged them several times into his chest and abdomen. Horrified, the family screamed and begged the soldiers to stop.

Finally the sergeant said, "Now you can bury him, if you wish."

We quickly retrieved the stones and covered the body. Then the Senegalese took us all to the French military headquarters, about twenty miles from Rachaya.

The burning of Rachaya and the massacre committed

by the Senegalese troops caused a great deal of protest in the recently formed League of Nations and around the world. Donations poured in to the local Red Cross from many countries, particularly from the United States and from Brazil and other Latin American nations where there were large Lebanese colonies. France was forced to acknowledge its unspeakable act and to contribute to the reconstruction of the town, which was totally rebuilt within two years.

2 · *Young Revolutionary*

WHO was Salem, my father, who led a short-lived revolution against French imperialism and lost his life tragically?

My father was a native of Lebanon, but he did not learn to love freedom and hate colonialism in his own country. He learned this in a far-distant land, which at that time used to be called "the Promised Land": the United States.

He was born in Rachaya. The exact date of his birth is not known, but it was probably around 1875. Rachaya was a small farming community nestled on the western slopes of Mount Hermon. At the time of the revolution, the town itself had almost 10,000 inhabitants and was divided into a lower and an upper part. The lower part was inhabited by the merchants; they lived in huts made of mud and wood. The roofs were flat, and in the winter they collected a lot of snow, which had to be shoveled frequently; this was one of my responsibilities when I was six years old. In the upper part of town, on a cliff surrounding the Elkaala, the homes were built of stone and brick; this was where the wealthy lived. The town was partly surrounded by farming terraces covered with grapevines, fruit trees, and wheat fields. The eastern section of the town looked toward the barren slope of Mount Hermon. From the upper part of the town and from the Elkaala can be seen the El Bekaa Valley and its farmlands. From the top of Mount Hermon there is a spectacular view; to the east are Damascus and the Syrian plains and desert; to the southeast, the Palestinian land now called Israel, and the Golan Heights; and to the west, the Bekaa plains, visible as far as Baalbek, Zahle, and Beirut.

The whole town was dominated by the huge Elkaala, whose history is obscure. It is believed that this fortress was built by the Romans, during their occupation of Syria, to dominate all of Lebanon, Syria, and Palestine. The Elkaala was considered by the Romans—as well as by the other nations that occupied the Middle East through the centuries—to be the "hub" of all Syria. It is built of massive stones in a high region, and it has nine or ten openings for observation along its circular front wall. This high wall made entry difficult, since there was but a single circular road, which led to the main entrance. It is thought that in Roman times a handful of troops inside the fortress could withstand the siege of many, provided they had food and water.

Located in the mountains, Rachaya would be covered by up to ten feet of snow in the winter, which gave the town a beautiful appearance but made it extremely difficult for the people to move about by their only means of transportation: mules and donkeys. In the spring and summer, the town and surrounding area would explode into all kinds of flowering trees and blooming vines with beautiful green leaves. A smell of ripening grapes and fruits, mixed with the smell of sheep and goat herds and the manure of cows, horses, and donkeys, could be detected several miles away.

The inhabitants of Rachaya were rugged mountaineers, mostly farmers who lived on what they raised. Some grew wheat and corn; others produced grapes, wines, and vegetables. There were those who had their own herds of cows, sheep, and goats; they were not only milk producers, but also butchers, who sold meat. There were very few educated professionals; in fact, in the whole town there were only one doctor and two lawyers.

When the grapes were harvested in the late summer and early fall, Rachaya burst into all kinds of activity. Some crushed the grapes to make wine, others distilled the liquor called "arrack," still others made a grape jam called "dibs." All these grape fermentations gave the town a distinctive odor at that season.

Despite their poor or modest standard of living, the inhabitants of Rachaya were a proud people. They considered themselves the legitimate inhabitants of Lebanon, who had fought in the past against the Ottoman Empire and now were fighting against French colonialism and enslavement. Perhaps this pride resulted from Rachaya's hard living conditions and rigorous mountain climate. Moreover, the fortress of Elkaala made the people feel that the town was impregnable and that they could resist any form of oppression.

The Lebanese living in the main cities—the Lebanese elite—looked on the inhabitants of Rachaya as the troublemakers, but also as the most rugged people of Lebanon. In fact, much of the resistance against the Ottoman Empire originated among the small group of men who lived in Rachaya and the surrounding area. These mountaineers soon became disillusioned with their new French masters and began to resent their arrogance, realizing that the Treaty of Versailles had only changed the guard.

My father was born to a poor and illiterate family in the slums of Rachaya during the Turkish occupation. His family owned a small vineyard and a herd of sheep and goats. From the vineyard they obtained raisins,

wine, arrack, and other staples, which they sold or used
in their home. From the sheep and goats they obtained
milk, cheese, butter, and meat for their butcher shop.
This business provided barely enough for survival.
Their home was a hut made of mud and timber; everyone slept in one large room on mattresses that were
placed on the floor and stored in a corner in the daytime.
Adjoining this room was a kitchen and storage area. The
cooking was done indoors only during the winter; at any
other time it took place outdoors, by burning wood or
charcoal. A mud barn housed the sheep and goats, and
one donkey served as transportation for the family. No
one in the town had running water, electricity, or sew-
age facilities. Water had to be brought in cans or jugs
from wells or streams four or five miles away by donkey
or carried on the heads of the women. At night, oil lamps
lit the homes. Sanitation did not exist, and diseases such
as typhoid fever, malaria, trachoma, tuberculosis, and
dysentery were rampant.

Besides my father, who was the eldest son, there were
four boys and four girls in the family. Early in life my
father demonstrated leadership, hard work, and responsibility. As the oldest boy he began helping his father and
mother by cultivating the land and tending the sheep
and goats. Although he did not have enough money to
go to school, he learned how to read and write Arabic
from a cousin who was the Catholic priest of Rachaya,
and who later provided much needed assistance to
Salem's family. When he was ten years old, he practically
assumed the leadership of the family. His brothers and
sisters were attacked early in life by the dreadful eye
disease trachoma, which in those days was prevalent in
the Middle East. By some miracle my father had only a
mild case. Every day he would rise at five o'clock and
take a herd of sheep and goats to the hills or plains to

graze. He would return with the herd late at night and then start preparing the next day's meat for the butcher shop. At night he would help his mother and father clean and bathe the eyes of his brothers and sisters with a solution prescribed by the eye doctor who passed through the town once a month.

During his childhood and youth my father learned of the horrible tortures and massacres committed by Turkish soldiers in the Arab countries. During his adolescence he saw with his own eyes how the Turks beat his friends and relatives—men, women, and children alike. He witnessed several rapes committed by Turks and knew that the authorities would not punish them. He developed a hatred for the Turkish regime and for all colonialism, but he knew of no solution.

One day he told his family that there was no way for him to improve their living conditions if he remained in Lebanon, that he had decided to seek another life in a distant land called America. He had managed to save enough money for a one-way ticket on a ship leaving the port of Beirut for the New World.

Years later he told us the story of his trip in steerage, where he lived with rats and cockroaches, ate miserably, and was seasick for the duration of the voyage.

Finally he reached the port of New York, entered the Promised Land, and promptly felt lost. He did not know anyone and could not speak a word of English, and he was penniless and overwhelmed and awed by the tall buildings and the crowded streets. Nevertheless, with his enormous willpower and with his mountaineer ruggedness, he was determined to succeed in his new life.

3 · *American Interlude*

WHEN my father arrived in America, he was about sixteen years old. His first night in New York was spent under a tree in a park. During the next few days, he was busy locating people of Arabic origin. He obtained a job as a dishwasher and cleaner in a restaurant belonging to an Arab immigrant. This job gave him free food, and the opportunity to earn some money and learn English—his two major goals. He spent hours each night memorizing the pronunciation of the English words for things like bread, dish, and spoon. His capacity for hard work, his eagerness to learn and to save, and his pleasant disposition led to better jobs at the restaurant.

Within about seven months he had saved enough money to send a few dollars to his family in Lebanon. Soon thereafter, he learned that the nucleus of an Arabic-speaking colony was forming in Springfield, Illinois. He continued to work in the restaurant until he saved enough money to go west. Then he bought the cheapest train ticket from New York to Chicago and traveled the rest of the way to Springfield on foot.

On meeting his compatriots in Springfield, he found that nearly all of them were poor like himself, and everyone was trying to survive as a peddler. The details of that profession, as told by his countrymen, fascinated him. He thought that peddling would make it possible for him to meet American farmers and their families, observe how the Americans managed their lives at home, and also learn English.

So he began his peddling career by gathering articles for sale from door to door in farming communities. He packed his merchandise, as well as his own clothes and food, into a huge bundle and traveled on foot all through Illinois, Indiana, and Michigan. Neither rain, snow, hostile people, nor wild animals ever frightened him. He slept in the open country, under a tree, or in the corner of a barn. He washed his clothes and bathed in streams and rivers. Because of his inherent good nature, his humility, and his apparent honesty, he was well received at the homes on whose doors he knocked. He sold his stock rapidly and then went to the nearest large town to replenish it. With his thrifty and modest habits, he saved most of his earnings and religiously sent some to his family in Lebanon.

He hungered to learn about America and its history. He saw people, white and black alike, working together freely, without any interference from armed sentries or police. Although he observed differences in the living conditions and treatment of whites and blacks, these never bothered him, because they were minor by comparison with the differences between the Turks and Arabs in his own country. He asked his customers how all this came about. How was this country able to liberate itself from English colonialism? How did a small band of American patriots gather enough force and courage to overthrow the powerful English?

By talking to people and reading a little, he learned about the revolt against the English, about George Washington and Thomas Jefferson. He learned that not too long ago the United States had gone through a tragic and destructive civil war. He was astonished to learn that the American president who witnessed this terrible holocaust was the son of poor peasant farmers—a man named Lincoln, who had lived in the same city, Springfield, where he, Salem, had started his peddling career. The sentence from his reading that he would repeat time and again to his fellow Lebanese, and with fervor, was Patrick Henry's famous line, "Give me liberty or give me death."

My father remained in the United States for about five years. He loved the country and everything that it stood for. He loved the sight of people farming their crops without interference and without fear of confiscation. He wanted to stay in the United States, but the news from his family in Lebanon was discouraging. His father had developed trachoma and become blind. One of his brothers had been stricken with tuberculosis and was gravely ill. The money my father was sending was not enough, particularly since the Turkish authorities took half in taxes.

Salem had saved $7,000—in those days a small fortune. He decided to return to Lebanon. He took the train back to New York, where he traded in his dollars for gold (the dollar was unknown in the Middle East at that time). He left on the same boat on which he had come five years before, again in the cheapest class. On arriving in Beirut, he changed back into the typical Arabic dress of the mountaineers. He rented a mule and headed for the mountains and his hometown of Rachaya.

4 · Life in Lebanon

ON his return Salem was received enthusiastically by everyone, but he found his family in extremely poor condition. He resumed the leadership of the family and had the doctor come from Beirut to treat his brothers and sisters. He bought farmland and vineyards, increased the herd of goats and sheep, began remodeling and enlarging the house, built another barn, and reopened his father's butcher shop. His business grew rapidly, and the health of his brothers and sisters improved. A year and a half after his return, his father died, leaving the family's affairs and problems entirely in Salem's hands. But Salem thrived on adversity. His new responsibilities injected new energy and determination into his actions.

Salem talked about America to anyone who would listen. A wonderful country, he would say, one could live there without interference from colonial authorities. Many of his friends, as well as three of his brothers, emigrated to the United States. The brothers started work in precisely those states where their eldest brother had started, though several years later they moved to western Canada. Salem's youngest brother, George, decided. to go to Brazil.

When he was about thirty years old, Salem married a distant relative, Suraya, who was thirteen or fourteen years old. On the day of the wedding in January 1902, a huge snowstorm hit the town, leaving ten or twelve feet of snow on the ground. The bride's father carried Suraya to the church. After the wedding, the bride and groom returned to Salem's home, which had now been emptied of all other occupants. The honeymoon lasted only one day; at five in the morning on the following day, Salem was back at work taking care of his herd and the butcher shop.

My mother was as hard-working and determined as my father. She immediately took charge of the household, though she never did learn how to read or write. She instituted a thrifty and disciplined regimen that lasted all her life. She became, and remained, the driving force behind the entire family.

After a year, Salem and Suraya had their first child, a girl. Two other girls and six boys followed, practically one a year; I was the third boy. Upon reaching the age of five or six, each child was assigned a job. My parents gave their children a perfect example of responsibility, working from 6:00 A.M. until 11:00 P.M. every day, including Saturday and Sunday. I recall vividly the frequent talks my father and mother had with us. The major theme was how to face life and perform one's duties with firmness and diligence, and without fear.

On the days when I was to take the herds to the mountains, my mother would awaken me at five. I would bring my lunch and stay with the sheep and goats, protected by my dog, until it began to get dark. Shepherding was my favorite work, and I found the lambing season in the spring especially exhilarating. We would take the herd to the field armed with baskets designed to carry newborn lambs and goats back home.

Many times I helped deliver the lambs. Some came out one foot first, the other foot stuck in the uterus. My father taught me how to insert my hand inside the uterus, extract the second leg, and pull the baby lamb out. I was also taught how to clean the mouth and the nose of the baby, how to get him to breathe, and how to help him to reach for his mother's milk. One of my biggest thrills was to return home with two or three healthy newborn lambs. Each season the competition between me and my brothers over how many newborns each of us would bring home was fierce.

When my two eldest sisters married, my father convinced them to leave Lebanon and financed their trip to the United States. They later moved to Canada. He wanted his boys to have an education similar to the one that impressed him so in the United States, and he convinced his cousin, the Catholic priest of the town, to open a school and hire teachers. My brothers and I made arrangements to go to school at least three days a week; the rest of the time we spent working in the butcher shop, herding the flocks, and helping the family earn a living.

When my eldest brother, Mussa, completed his preliminary education and was about twelve years old, my father persuaded him to go to the New World. Instead of emigrating to the United States, however, Mussa chose to go to Brazil, where my youngest uncle, George, had established himself fairly well.

My father was eager to improve the social conditions in Rachaya and to apply some of the technical knowledge he had learned in America. But his dreams of improving his community and continuing to thrive in business were shattered by the holocaust of World War I. The Ottoman Empire, which ruled the Middle East, joined Germany against France, England, and their allies. The Turkish authorities drafted young men of military age and sent them to Anatolia to serve in the Turkish army.

My father saw many of his friends and relatives packed in horse-drawn carts or driven like cattle and marched off to military camps. He, however, had no intention of being sacrificed for the glory of the Ottoman Empire, and he escaped to the mountains, where he lived as a fugitive for almost four years. He hid in caves and other spots on Mount Hermon. Occasionally he would visit his family after midnight, when he was absolutely sure it was safe. The Turkish soldiers looked for him everywhere, but without success. During his absence my mother and the children kept the business going, though at a much slower pace.

At the end of World War I, my father reappeared in Rachaya and again took charge of the business, which began to thrive as before. During the postwar international negotiations my father had great hopes that Lebanon, along with other countries of the Middle East, would be given its freedom. He followed the debates at Versailles with much interest and was certain that Wilson, the great American president, would persuade the other powers to free Lebanon. But alas, his dreams were shattered. The Sykes-Picot Agreement divided the Middle East among the victors—France, Great Britain, and Russia. Lebanon went to France.

My father, disillusioned, fell into despair. He and his friends stood in the streets, broken-hearted and with tears in their eyes, witnessing the departure of the Turkish troops and the coming of the French, hating both. As he watched the lowering of the Turkish flag and the raising of the French flag, he asked some of his fellow Lebanese, "What does all this mean? One colonial power has simply replaced another."

Soon they found out that the new colonial power was just as ruthless as the earlier one, if not more so. The French established a huge military base, equipped with artillery and machine guns, about twenty miles from Rachaya. Furthermore, they began brainwashing the population of Lebanon by establishing Jesuit schools, which were nothing but an arm of the French government, designed to convert the Lebanese youth into French slaves. My father managed to suppress his disillusionment and his hatred of French colonialism by working hard in his vineyards and his shop. Nevertheless, he could not help preaching that Lebanon and Syria and the entire Middle East would someday be free of colonialism.

An incident occurred in 1923 that was to have a great impact on his life. His youngest sister was nursing her two-month-old baby one day near a well at her home. A French soldier approached and asked her to pull up a bucket of water so that he could wash his face and refresh himself. She told him that he was more than welcome to pull up the water himself, but that she was unable to do it because she was nursing her baby. Without a word of warning, the French soldier aimed his gun and fired. The helpless woman was killed instantly, the baby dropping near her body.

Her family and the neighbors rushed to the site and became hysterical. A messenger notified my father, who was in his vineyard. When he saw his favorite sister dead, lying in a pool of blood, he turned pale, in agony. Later, as her coffin was being lowered into the grave, he promised his sister that he would take care of her family and that he would avenge her death, no matter what the consequences.

Feeling that life could not continue in such a state of slavery, he organized the nucleus of a revolutionary force to fight the French army. He traveled on foot, mostly at night, to the villages near Rachaya and to the other towns, explaining, exhorting, and instilling a love of freedom among his countrymen. He told them how a small band of Americans was able to defeat the powerful British army and navy.

These clandestine meetings continued, with the aim of organizing groups and gathering weapons, which were mostly stolen from the French. By late 1924 my father thought he had enough support for a successful uprising. On that fateful day in 1925 when he and his followers stormed the Elkaala and overcame the French garrison, he thought his dreams were finally being realized.

But he had misjudged the power of the nearby colonial army, as well as the desire for revolution among the inhabitants of the major cities. Toward the end he realized that this misjudgment would cost him his life and bring misery and destruction to his family, his followers, and his town.

5 · Prison-Camp Years

THROUGHOUT the twenty-mile night march to French headquarters, the Senegalese soldiers constantly humiliated, insulted, and kicked the members of Salem's family, particularly the older boys. On the march were Salem's old mother, his wife, Suraya, his daughter Frieda, and his boys Issa, Anis, Fawzi, Nassery, and I. Issa and I were beaten badly, often with rifle butts. Finally, in the early-morning hours, we reached the prison camp.

The French headquarters occupied a vast area on the Bekaa Plain between the towns of Zahle and Baalbek. There were many buildings and barracks, and a wide-open area that served for military training and exercise. The prison camp was located in a swampy area heavily infested with mosquitoes, about two miles from the main headquarters. It was isolated from everything by a barbed-wire fence. The camp had some old wooden barracks intermingled with huts of mud. Each barrack consisted of one large room where prisoners slept on thin mattresses on the floor. At night bedbugs crawled in and around the beds, and the inhabitants of the camp would get up and spend hours hunting them by the light of oil lamps.

In a small area located between every four huts stood a rectangular wooden box that covered a large pit in the ground. This served as a toilet facility. Next to this so-called toilet there was a large pit for cooking. The water supply consisted of two public faucets that provided water for the whole camp. Baths were allowed once a month. The prisoners suffered from lice and a variety of skin diseases.

When we reached the camp, the Senegalese placed us in the oldest barrack, which had no floor. The mattresses were laid directly on the dirt. Since we were exhausted from the long march and the beating, we all fell asleep as soon as we lay down. For three days we saw no one. On the fourth day a French soldier came to tell us that we would be informed about our fate in due time, and that anyone attempting to leave the camp would be shot on the spot.

Finally, in the fifth week of our detention, a soldier announced that we could have visitors. Soon we began to see relatives from the neighboring villages. They were allowed to bring us some food, but not to talk to us for more than a few minutes. Then, about two and a half months after our arrest, we had work assigned us. My mother and sister were to clean the soldiers' barracks and wash their clothes; Issa and I were to clean the latrines, shine the officers' boots, and work as servants in the officers' quarters and mess hall. The other children were too small for any work, and my grandmother was too old.

After some months my uncle who had been Rachaya's priest, and was now the Archbishop of Baalbek, inter-vened with the French authorities to allow the children to go to the Jesuit school. At the end of the first year my oldest brother and I were allowed to go to the school, which was located near the military headquarters. Dur-ing the trip to and from school, Issa and I started plan-ning his escape. This idea required a great deal of thought. If Issa escaped, he would have to leave the country; otherwise he would be shot.

One day we discussed the matter with my mother. She promptly agreed and promised to speak with some relatives who were coming to visit us that night. Her fertile mind was working already. During the visiting hour she told one of our relatives about the plan. He was to arrange for a Brazilian visa. When this was ready, Issa was to escape, disguised as a woman, and head directly for Beirut and the boat to Brazil.

The plan unfolded like clockwork. On the designated day a crowd of relatives came to visit us, mostly women. When Issa left with them, dressed as a woman, the sentries did not notice. A car took him to Beirut, where another relative was waiting with the visa and boat ticket. Three hours after his escape, Issa left Lebanon. So, at ten years of age, I became the head of the family.

After Issa's escape, surveillance of my family became much stricter. For a long time we were not allowed to receive visitors, and I was sent back to work in the mess hall. After several months I was allowed to return to the Jesuit school, though under close supervision.

The Jesuits were agents of the French authorities, and their treatment of the students varied. Those whose parents were considered revolutionaries and anti-French were treated in the cruelest way. For the slightest reason, such as arriving late for early mass or missing weekly communion, students were whipped with an elephant tail, were forced to kneel, with bare knees, on pebbles for hours, and were not allowed any food for the whole day.

After Issa's departure, I was the only one in the family going to the Jesuit school, since the other boys were too young. I quickly came to hate the brainwashing of the Jesuit priests. Often I missed early mass, particularly in the winter. I had no shoes to protect my feet from the snow, nor any desire to go to church or to weekly confession and communion. I became an atheist. I said to myself, "If this is the way God treats people who worship him and hide in his church, then he doesn't know what justice is! So I don't want to have anything to do with him." The more this idea became stamped on my mind, the more I hated the Jesuits and the more often I missed mass, confession, and communion. This brought more punishment, more beatings. My war with the Jesuits escalated enormously in the year and a half I attended their school. The situation reached the point where I ran away from school almost every day. Finally I was expelled and ordered back to hard labor in the sanitary division.

The so-called sanitary division, or hospital, of the French military camp was probably the most unsanitary part of the whole compound. It consisted of filthy old barracks, each containing about eight rusted metal cots with flat springs of woven wires covered by a blanket. On the floor between the cots lay thin old mattresses, to be used when the cots were filled. Bedbugs, flies, mosquitoes, and cockroaches could be seen everywhere. This hospital was used only for prisoners, since French soldiers were sent to better hospitals in Beirut. Next to the barracks there was the usual single latrine, consisting of a rectangular wooden structure four by eight feet, covering a large hole in the ground that served as a cesspool. To defecate, one would squat over a hole in the wooden board that formed the base of the box. No disinfectant or chemicals of any kind were ever added to the cesspool. When the hole became filled with feces and urine, it was covered with dirt and the wooden structure was moved to another hole already dug in the ground. Sometimes holes were dug near the well, which led to frequent outbreaks of typhoid fever. Most of the patients admitted to this hospital were terminal cases of typhoid fever, malaria, or dysentery.

My first job following my expulsion from school, at twelve years of age, was to dig holes for the cesspools. I would rise every morning at 6:00 A.M., eat something, and, while the weather was still cool, start digging. When the hole became very deep, my youngest brother, Anis, was allowed to help me remove the dirt. The dirt was piled up near the hole, so that it could be used to cover the cesspool when it was filled. It took two weeks to dig each hole and get it ready for use. Covering the cesspool holes and cleaning the floor of the hospital barracks were also among my duties.

I had been working in this filthy job for about six months when Fawzi, one of my younger brothers, became ill. His disease started with vomiting and diarrhea, then high fever, incredible sweating, and severe abdominal pains. We called the doctor, who diagnosed typhoid fever. He advised us to give Fawzi no food and only a few sips of water. He suggested that we move him to the hospital, but, knowing the conditions of that place, I refused. I told the doctor and the authorities that we would keep him in our barracks and care for him there.

Every day Fawzi's condition became worse. We were totally frustrated, because we could not do anything to help him. We were not allowed to call a private physician, even though the one available in the camp did nothing.

One day the poor boy gave a loud scream, held his abdomen with his hand, and expelled a large quantity of blood with his watery stool. Shortly thereafter he became unconscious, and within twenty-four hours he was dead. He was only six. Much later I learned that these were symptoms of bowel perforations, which in those days were frequent complications of typhoid fever.

The death of my young brother increased our despair and our hatred of the oppressive military regime that dominated our lives and which we held responsible for Fawzi's death. We kept saying to ourselves that had we been free, we could have called a good doctor, who might have saved the boy. These thoughts tortured us for a long time after we buried Fawzi near the camp.

One day about eight months after my expulsion from school I was told by the officer in charge to report to the pharmacy. The pharmacy was located in a small store next to the main headquarters building, in the cleanest and best-kept section of the camp. I was to learn shortly that this privileged condition was largely the result of the pharmacist's influence. He was a demanding and forceful Italian who, over the years, had accumulated a great deal of prestige and influence through cunning and intrigue. He knew the French authorities would have a hard time finding another person for the job, so he got whatever he asked for, including extra help to keep his place clean.

When I presented myself to this stern, unsmiling pharmacist, he told me I was to wash the glassware, scrub the floors, and keep the shelves neat. He immediately dismissed me by saying, "Get to work." Much later I found out that I had gotten this job through secret negotiations between my uncle the Archbishop and the French commander.

The pharmacy had a few drugs imported from France. Most of its business was devoted to filling prescriptions, written by the pharmacist himself or by one of the doctors, for such illnesses as malaria, dysentery, respiratory infections, syphilis, and gonorrhea. Since medical practice in those days was rather primitive, the pharmacy stock was largely composed of ingredients to make paregoric elixir, cough syrup, quinine capsules, arsenic solu-

tions for syphilis, potassium permanganate for gonorrhea, and ointments of various kinds for skin diseases.
The preparation of a large number of prescriptions required much glassware. Since this was scarce, I had to
wash the same batch over and over.

From the outset I gave my heart, soul, and energy to
my job and to the pharmacist. He not only dispensed the
drugs but also treated the majority of the patients, including many soldiers and officers with gonorrhea and
syphilis. Gonorrhea at that time was treated by daily
irrigations, using solutions of potassium permanganate.
Syphilis was treated by intravenous injections of arsenic
preparations every two or three days. The pharmacist
accumulated power because he knew what skeletons
each patient had in his closet. I decided that my first job
was to cultivate his friendship and goodwill. When I had
some extra time, I went to the shelves and memorized the
names of the drugs. I observed closely how the pharmacist measured ingredients and made the elixirs or the
quinine capsules. Pretending that I was cleaning the area
around the couch on which a patient was lying, I
watched carefully how the pharmacist performed genital irrigations on the soldiers and officers.

The pharmacist was married but had a mistress on the
side. I soon became the confidential messenger employed
by all three—the man, the wife, and the mistress. And so,
within six months I had gained the full confidence of the
pharmacist. He gave me the key to the pharmacy and
permission to open the place and close it any time I liked.
I would begin working around 6:00 A.M., and by 9:00
A.M., when the pharmacist arrived, everything in the
shop was clean and in its proper place.

One day the news came of a severe outbreak of malaria
in the Bekaa Valley. Soon diseased patients began arriving, and the hospital barracks were filled up in no time.

So the pharmacist asked the French authorities to send one or two doctors from Beirut or some other large city. Two days later a young doctor arrived. After being briefed on the situation, he asked for 2,000 capsules of quinine, to take with him, so that he could treat the patients in their homes.

The job of preparing the quinine capsules was entrusted to me. I saw in it a chance to prove my capability and improve my status in the eyes of the pharmacist. I worked the whole day and most of the night to get the capsules ready for the following day. The pharmacist was with his mistress all that time. He was pleased indeed when he arrived the next morning and found all the capsules ready.

The young doctor who was going to the Bekaa Valley needed an assistant to help him see the patients, give them the right number of quinine capsules, and instruct them how to take them. I was selected to accompany the doctor and was thrilled by this opportunity to visit the world outside. For almost three months the doctor and I rode every morning in a horse-drawn carriage to the various houses and communities to examine the sick patients. During this association I learned a great deal about medicine, including the use of the thermometer, stethoscope, reflex hammer, and other devices for examining the sick. Most of all, I began to feel a love for medicine and a compassion for the sick and helpless patients. Occasionally I witnessed a patient during the malaria crisis, with its severe chills and shivering, chattering teeth and trembling limbs, followed by fever and sweating. I sat at these patients' sides, observing the symptoms meticulously, and did not leave until the crisis had passed.

I continued to work in the pharmacy and to assist the doctors whenever they needed me for about six years.

During this time the pharmacist became like a father to me. He not only treated me with kindness, but also taught me a great deal about pharmaceutical work, including drug effects, treatment of venereal and other diseases, and salesmanship. He also confided all his family problems to me, including the delicate balance between loyalty to his wife and infatuation with his mistress. During the last three years of my work in the pharmacy, I practically ran the whole business, including the treatment of soldiers and officers with gonorrhea, a job in which I became proficient.

During that time the pharmacist and my uncle the Archbishop interceded with the French authorities on behalf of my family. Consequently, from 1928 on, our living conditions improved considerably. We were given decent quarters and were allowed to receive visitors and to visit relatives outside the camp.

6 · Liberation

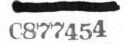

AT seven o'clock in the morning on December 1, 1932, a messenger arrived summoning me to appear before the commanding officer an hour later. The night before, a heavy snow had fallen. Then in the early morning the sun appeared from behind the clouds, and its bright rays on the still-unspoiled layer of white snow were a heavenly sight.

This early-morning summons from the commander was most unusual for several reasons. First, I had seen him the day before in the pharmacy. He came to "buy" a bottle of perfume for his mistress. Confidentially, he told me that he wanted a fragrance different from his wife's. Since his wife usually got Coty, I suggested Houbigant. When he made a gesture to pay and could not "find" his wallet, I told him I would list the bottle as having been broken accidentally. He grinned broadly and left.

Shortly thereafter, his wife came in to buy some cough syrup for the children. I charged her a low price as a courtesy. So when I received the summons the following morning, a cold shiver ran down my spine: perhaps his wife had discovered the perfume destined for the mistress, and the commander suspected me of having tipped her off.

The distance from our barracks to the commander's

office was about five hundred feet, and I usually made it in less than three minutes. But on that early December morning I wished it would take the whole day. Nevertheless, precisely at 8:00 A.M. I was at the door, and the armed guard escorted me into the office. The commander sat behind his desk, going over some papers in a large folder. Without looking at me, and for the first time in my seven years of confinement, he asked me to sit down. I felt a little relieved, because I thought he was extending me a courtesy in exchange for the service I had performed for him the day before. However, when he continued fiddling with the papers, a cold sweat started seeping from every pore of my skin.

After several minutes of tense silence he finally looked at me and smiled. "Nick," he said, "I have good news for you and your family. We just received orders from General Headquarters in Beirut to set you and your family free. Within the next twenty-four hours!" He paused, and for the next two minutes he stared at my pale, stunned face. "The orders further state," he continued, "that you and your family are to leave for any country of your choice within the next seven days."

He fell silent, and again we stared at each other: he the master, more than twice my age, who for seven years had held me and my family in constant fear and terror; and I the slave, who for those seven years had tried every trick, legal and illegal, to ensure our survival. Then suddenly I started sobbing as I had never sobbed before, not even during my father's brutal death and mutilation.

The commander got up slowly, put his hand on my shoulder, and pressed it lightly. He then silently walked away, closed the door behind him, and left me to my thoughts.

For many years I wondered why I had been so upset. Why did I cry so much? Was it because we were finally free? Was it because we were to leave our country, for which my father and one of my brothers had died in vain, or because of the uncertainties about the future? Was it because I was to leave behind people such as the pharmacist and the doctor, whom I first had feared but later came to love and respect? These questions troubled me for many years. Only much later, when I read Tolstoy's *War and Peace* for the second or third time, was I able to find solace. In the chapter where he analyzes the many causes and events that led to the War of 1812, with its crime, theft, corruption, and treason, Tolstoy ends with a fatalistic question: "When an apple falls from a tree, why does it fall?"

I left the commander's office and walked slowly over the snow-covered ground to our barracks. My mother was doing her usual washing, my grandmother was cooking, and my sister was cleaning the floor. I gathered them around me and broke the news. They were as stunned as I was and also began to cry. After a few minutes I calmed them down and conveyed to them the urgency of the matter: we had to leave the camp within twenty-four hours and the country within seven days.

There were two major obstacles that had to be dealt with immediately: raising money to buy tickets and finding a country that would accept us and give us a visa on such short notice.

I had some savings from my work in the pharmacy, but they were hardly enough to buy a one-way ticket for one person, let alone for the whole family. We thought of appealing to our relatives in North and South America, but 1932 was no time to ask people for money. We had seen photographs of poor people in the United States waiting in long lines for food.

So I decided to turn to my uncle the Archbishop, in Baalbek, which was about twenty-five miles from our camp. I got there in no time, with the help of a relative who operated a primitive taxi service. At Baalbek I was awed by the pomp and ceremony that surround an archbishop. His building was the largest I had ever seen, and the luxury of its interior left me speechless. Everywhere there were tapestries, paintings, elaborate furniture, and other signs of wealth.

I presented myself to the guard at the gate, who was dressed in a colorful uniform and had a long sword hanging at one side. I told him I wanted to see my uncle on a matter of great urgency. Half an hour later I was conducted to a room inside the residence and told that I would not be able to see His Excellency until dinnertime. I sat down on the edge of a bed, nervously biting my fingernails. My uncle had been extremely embarrassed when I was expelled from the Jesuit school. He and I had had hot arguments at the time; he had wanted me to return to the school, and I had refused. I had seen him but rarely since that time. I hoped that, because the incident had occurred more than six years before, our differences would have been forgotten by now. But on that December day, in his palace, I could not help but wonder whether my difficulty in seeing him promptly meant punishment for past behavior. Be that as it may, there was nothing I could do but wait.

Soon a messenger came to my room and said that His Excellency had commanded him to show me the city, its majestic Roman temples and magnificent colonnades. Although I could not but admire these ancient works of art, my mind was fixed on other, more pressing matters.

We returned to the residence around five in the afternoon and I was told to get ready for dinner, which would begin promptly at six at the sound of the bell. I was then shown to a room where for the first time in my life I saw a modern toilet and a bathtub. I confess that the sight of the bathroom gave me more of a thrill than the whole palace. I sat on a toilet seat for the first time in my life; I remained sitting there, enjoying myself, unaware of the time until I heard the bell ringing. Then I got up, straightened my clothes, and rushed to the dining room, thinking I was to dine with my uncle alone. I was flabbergasted when I found more than fifteen clergymen, of all ranks, each standing behind his chair awaiting His Excellency. There were two servants, one of whom showed me to my chair. Five minutes later His Excellency entered. All of the priests bowed, and I walked toward him, took his hand, and kissed it. He patted me on the head and asked if I had enjoyed my tour of the city.

After a short prayer in Latin, everyone sat down and the dinner was served. I kept looking at my uncle. He was attired in a red velvet robe embroidered with gold, and the cap on his head was of the same material. The table gleamed with porcelain dishes, crystal, and silver. We had a well-prepared five-course dinner, the food such as I had never eaten before. The priests and the servants treated my uncle like a king.

Since I was not accustomed to such luxury and knew nothing of table manners, I decided to imitate a young priest sitting next to me. The dinner lasted more than two hours, at the end of which I was literally soaked in sweat. Finally my uncle rose, and everyone else did the same. He signaled for me to follow him to his study.

"What brings you here?" he asked, closing the door.

I repeated all that the commander of the camp had conveyed to me and explained that we still had to find money for the tickets and a country that would give us a visa. He told me with a smile that he knew all about it, but did not say how. Many years later I learned that he had been instrumental in securing our release through his influence with the Vatican and the French government.

Anyway, he offered to lend us half of the price of the tickets; the other half would have to come from our relatives in America and Brazil, he said. He then sent night letters to my sisters and their husbands, and to my uncles and brothers, asking them urgently to send money for our travel.

I thanked him, kissed his hand, and asked permission to return to my family. He urged me to stay overnight, but I convinced him that my presence with the family was imperative. He ordered his chauffeur to take me back to the camp. Just as I was about to leave, he put his hand on my shoulder, looked me in the eye, and said, "Nick, I have confidence that, whatever the future may hold, you will succeed." Then I saw two tears roll down his withered cheeks. He and I knew that this was the last time we would see each other. We continued to correspond until 1937, when he died of diabetes; his death occurred on the very day I entered medical school.

Twenty-four hours after I got back to my family, we moved out of the camp and stayed with some relatives in the city of Zahle. I went to Beirut to try to get visas from the American consul. When he learned that we had just been released from the military camp, he said that under no circumstances could we enter the United States. Neither the appeal of our sisters and uncles who were American citizens nor the intervention of our uncle as the Pope's representative in Lebanon was of any use.

Then I went to the Brazilian consulate. The consul said that, since we had relatives in Brazil who would be responsible for our support, he would grant visas to all of us. Forty-eight hours later, money for the tickets arrived from Brazil and the United States. Our departure was scheduled for December 10, 1932, on the Italian ship *Julius Caesar*.

The women of the family had meanwhile been busy preparing food for the journey. In Arab countries at that time it was the custom, whenever someone was to travel by mule, horse, or boat, to prepare special homemade pies with spices that could withstand a journey of one month or more without deteriorating. This habit remained with my mother all her life, even after I had become an established scientist and was traveling first-class in airplanes.

When we embarked in Beirut, the family's baggage consisted of a single trunk, containing our clothes, and several ten-gallon tin cans of the famous pies, despite my protest.

Fourth class on the *Julius Caesar* was a memorable experience. There were about 120 cots arranged as triple-deckers, without any concern for sanitation or hygiene. Rats, cockroaches, and bedbugs were there for all to see. Two toilets were provided for the entire fourth class—one for women and the other for men. The food was no better than what we had had during our worst period in the military camp, so we were thankful we had the pies.

The boat weighed anchor at 7:00 P.M. on December 10. We said good-bye to Lebanon with tears in our eyes. We thought it was the last time we would see our country, a prediction that turned out to be true for everyone except me. I did return in 1962 to search, unsuccessfully, for the place where we buried my father.

After short stops at Cyprus and Brindisi, at the tip of the Italian boot, we traveled north through the Adriatic Sea to Trieste. This was the roughest part of the trip. Strong, freezing winds and huge waves hit the ship from all sides, making it roll and pitch like a tiny object on the raging sea. Practically every passenger was seasick.

We remained in port for three days, with the first, second, and third classes put up in hotels and the fourth class quartered in storage barracks along the docks. On the fourth day the sea became calmer, so the *Julius Caesar* sailed south through the Adriatic and rounded the tip of the boot to reach Naples.

On the day after the ship left Naples, hell broke loose: an outbreak of gonorrhea among the men, particularly those of the upper classes. It was labeled "the Trieste epidemic." Complaints about purulent urethral discharge could be heard everywhere, along with obscene remarks and violent arguments. The situation became chaotic when the men found out how bad the medical facilities were on the ship: one small infirmary attended by a young doctor and a nurse, who were equipped for emergency accidents such as cuts, bruises, and sprains, but not for an epidemic of gonorrhea.

When I heard about the outbreak, I immediately saw a chance to improve our life during the trip. I went to the infirmary, told the doctor about my experience in the military camp in treating gonorrhea, and demonstrated my abilities on a man with a severe purulent discharge. The doctor promptly reported my expertise to the captain, and I was asked to work in the infirmary throughout the voyage. I accepted the offer on one condition— that my family and I be given comfortable accommodations at no extra cost. Our move was a celebration.

I went to work immediately; even though the infirmary was small, I managed to install four irrigation setups so that four men could be treated simultaneously. I asked the captain to purchase a large quantity of potassium permanganate in Gibraltar, our next stop, which he did. When we passed through the strait into the vastness of the Atlantic, life became comfortable and routine. Every day at 8:00 A.M. I reported to the infirmary, where a long line of men waited to be relieved of their purulent discharge. Irrigations continued until six or seven in the evening. Thereafter, only emergency cases were treated. Most of the victims were single, but three or four were married men accompanied by their wives. This created a delicate problem, because I had to impose abstention from sexual intercourse. The men asked me to tell their wives, which I did. For the rest of the voyage, I had to act as urologist for the men and as psychiatrist for their wives.

In no time I became known as the "good plumber," a label that brought me not only a great deal of respect and friendship, but also quite a lot of money in tips. Our last night on the ship was a great farewell party organized by the many patients I had treated, as well as by the doctor and his nurse; all had become my friends. The captain wished me luck with a glass of champagne.

Part Two

BRÁZIL

7 · School at Last

ON the morning of the last day of 1932, the *Julius Caesar* docked at Santos. Our relatives were waiting for us. It was an occasion charged with emotion.

I had little recollection of my brother Mussa, because I had been so young when he left Lebanon for Brazil. But I remembered Issa very well because we had shared the tragedies of Rachaya. We were both amazed, however, by the differences that seven years had made in our appearance. For me, Issa the teen-ager had become a man; for him, the boy he had left in charge of the family had grown up and become a young man full of energy. Four months after my arrival in Brazil, I turned seventeen.

We took the bus from Santos to São Paulo. Everyone was excited about meeting relatives we hardly knew, about being free at last in a new country, and we were stimulated by hope for the future.

My two oldest brothers worked as salesclerks in the small children's clothing store that belonged to my Uncle George. They were on fixed salaries, living in a boardinghouse and eating their meals either there or in restaurants. Their salaries were hardly sufficient to support them, let alone the newly arrived family. Uncle George, on the other hand, was considered to be relatively wealthy. He had made his fortune, I learned later, not in the small store that sold baby clothes, but by lending money at huge interest rates and manipulating mortgages and businesses that went bankrupt. He prospered until his death, in 1969, without ever having an office or a secretary. He was married and had one daughter, Yvonne, who was about my age and whom he worshipped. Every step he took, every nickel he made, and every piece of real estate he acquired, was to secure the future of Yvonne, her children, and her grandchildren.

Shortly after we settled in a rented shack in São Paulo, my brothers moved in with us and my mother assumed the leadership of the family. I was ordered to begin working in my uncle's store with my brothers. My two youngest brothers were too young to work, so they were sent to school. My mother took charge of all our finances, using only common sense, since she was ignorant of the most elementary arithmetic. She dictated the rules about personal allowances, rent, home expenses, clothes, food. She made it a law for all of us that at least a quarter of everyone's salary had to be saved and placed in the savings account in the bank at the end of each month—and heaven help anyone who disobeyed that law. She continued to be a powerful force in all our lives up to her death.

My first job in the store was selling clothes for infants. This gave me an opportunity to meet people and learn Portuguese. With my knowledge of French, I learned the new language quickly. My uncle and brothers saw, however, that I was not very efficient and productive, so they put a man on with me to teach me the art of salesmanship. After a few months, the man told my uncle that I would never make a good salesman. He was correct. More than half the customers I served left the store without buying anything. This infuriated my uncle, my mother, and my brothers. After a while they gave up trying to make me a salesman and changed my job to assistant to the cashier, and later to main cashier. Although this job appealed to me a little more, I knew that it was temporary. The idea of going to school and becoming a doctor had been brewing in my mind while I was on the ship. It gained momentum while my family was trying to make me a businessman. I was waiting only for the appropriate time to announce it to a family that was totally committed to business and cared little about anything else.

After I had been working some months in the store, Uncle George decided to go on an extended tour of the United States and Canada. He appointed me his representative in the store as well as in his private moneylending business. He handed me a stack of promissory notes, from all kinds of people—businessmen, farmers, doctors, teachers—who owed him money, and instructed me on how to collect the money, and if necessary how to begin bankruptcy proceedings and confiscate property. At the end of his enthusiastic talk, I was dumbfounded. Finally, I took the stack of notes and told him I would do my best.

The first note that fell due after he left was that of a doctor whose name I prefer not to mention, because the mere thought of my action toward him increases my guilt and makes me feel ashamed even after all these years. My oldest brother told me that this doctor was the most humane man in the city and that over seventy percent of his patients, particularly those of Syrian or Lebanese origin, were never charged anything, not even the price of drugs. He further told me that my uncle's interest rate ranged from twenty-five to seventy-five percent. But I ignored my brother's advice, because I was eager to please my uncle.

On the day the promissory note was due, I went to the doctor's office and confronted him with that dreadful piece of paper. He blushed, told me he did not have the

money, and asked for a thirty-day extension. I told him
I had no authority to grant him one, and that I would
give the note to the attorney and confiscate his office. He
looked me in the eye for two minutes, then smiled in a
way that I cannot describe and said, "Ask your brothers
and relatives how much they have paid during the past
several years for their medical care."

I left his office bewildered and unhappy. At the store
I told my oldest brother what had happened. "What do
you plan to do next?" he asked. "I plan to take the note
to the lawyer," I answered. In a short time a big crowd
of my relatives and other Syrians and Lebanese poured
into the store and almost lynched me. Some of them had
been alerted by my brother; others had been told by the
doctor's nurse. As a result, I told my brother to tell the
doctor that I was not going to do anything about it.

One month later I became ill, and that same good
doctor came to our home and took care of me. When I
offered to pay, he declined. I took the occasion to apolo-
gize personally for my action. We became friends, and
we remained so even after I left for the United States.
Whenever I returned to Brazil, I always called on him.
He continued to be our family physician and took care
of both my mother and Uncle George in their terminal
illnesses.

One week after the episode in the doctor's office, another promissory note fell due—that of a small farmer
living on the outskirts of São Paulo. I called him on the
phone and asked him if I could collect the money after
dinner. He hesitated briefly, then said yes and hung up.
I had a premonition that something was wrong; nevertheless, I took the streetcar and went to see him. He lived
about a third of a mile from the last stop. When I arrived
at the gate, he was standing at the door with a rifle in his
hand and a huge dog next to him. Before I touched the

gate, he yelled, "If you take one more step, you'll be dead," and he let the dog loose.

I turned around and started running as fast as I could. I did not stop until I was safely inside the streetcar that was to carry me back to the city. Exhausted and disgusted, I made up my mind to put an end to my job as my uncle's bill collector. Later I learned that the poor farmer had been milked of money several times the value of the note, but my uncle considered all that to be "interest." When I got home I went straight to bed.

The next morning I wrote to my uncle that I was unable to collect anything and could no longer continue with the job. Two weeks later I received a wire from him asking me to turn the notes over to an attorney friend of his, and this I gladly did.

The evening after the episode with the farmer, while all the family were gathered for dinner, I announced that I was going to continue my education and eventually become a doctor. A stunned silence followed. Then my mother exploded. She argued that I was leaving the business in which we were doing well, that eventually the store would be ours, and that my brothers needed me; also, that education was a waste of time, and I would starve. She then proceeded to give me dozens of examples of wealthy Lebanese and Syrians who never went to school and made large fortunes in business. The rest of the family echoed her sentiments. But I was adamant: "I have made up my mind and no one can change it but me." This did not stop my mother from lamenting my decision. She continued doing so even after I had become an established scientist. She always thought I could make more money in business than in medicine, and in that respect she was right.

After I had opened the store the following morning, my oldest brother, Mussa, who seemed sympathetic, took me aside and said: "There are night schools here that prepare students for universities. I know the director of one that is two blocks from here. Why not talk to him?"

"Why not indeed?" I said, and we walked the two blocks and he introduced me to the man who ran a small night school. The curriculum, as I realize now, was no different from any college preparatory curriculum in the United States, except that it was broader and considerably more conventional. I asked the director if I could attend some of the classes before I registered, so that I could assess my capacity to undertake such a formidable task. He gave me permission to audit any class of my choice for sixty days.

After a ten-day survey of all the subjects given at that school, I found I was deficient in mathematics, physics, the history of Brazil and other American nations, and Portuguese and Brazilian literature. But I was quite advanced in the biological sciences, world history, world literature, geography, and foreign languages. I figured out that, with the exception of mathematics and physics, I could make up the deficiencies by myself, since I found the other subjects easy. So I decided to register and concentrate at first on math, physics, and Portuguese.

My work in the store continued as before. I established a rigid daily schedule. I got up around 5:00 A.M. and studied until 7:00, then I ate a quick breakfast and went by streetcar to open the store. I worked in the store until 6:00 P.M., using every free moment during the day to study. I had supper near the store, and at 6:30 I was at the school. Classes began at 7:00 and continued until 10:00. After school I went home and studied until 1:00 A.M.

In a very short time, I was totally thrilled by the schoolwork and my growing education. Soon my younger brother Anis decided to work in the store after he finished high school. This relieved me from going early to open the store, and I had more time to study.

Four months after I started school, I had established a close friendship with three other students who were all my age and had economic problems similar to mine. One lived in a boardinghouse, but his room was separate from the main house and was located near a chicken coop. The four of us decided to make that room our collective study center from 10:00 P.M. until 1:00 A.M. Every night after school we went there by streetcar. We began studying promptly, each of us teaching the others a subject in which he was more proficient. Very often we departed from our required studies to argue about philosophy, national and international politics, social problems, theology, and mathematics. Those were the best years of my life, not only because they gave me the education I needed to enter the university, but also because they opened my eyes to the political and social problems Brazil was facing.

The government of Brazil at that time was headed by the ruthless dictator Getulio Vargas, who was supported by the military. Individual freedom and freedom of the press hardly existed. Each state was headed by a governor appointed or dismissed at will by the dictator. Both the central and the state governments were controlled by a police apparatus.

In Brazil, as in most Latin American countries, the students were the first to go on strike or start trouble whenever the people were dissatisfied with the government. In those days the law students were the spearhead of political upheaval. One day in 1934 the university students decided to strike against one of Vargas's decrees imposing further restrictions on freedom. They were soon joined by other students, including those from our school and from the high schools.

I joined the revolutionary force. We organized a silent march of thousands of students in the downtown area. Every student was to have a handkerchief in his mouth and his hands tied behind his back as symbols of oppression and the lack of freedom of speech. This protest began at 10:00 A.M. and was led by the organizers, including me. The marchers had hardly gone two hundred yards before they were surrounded by trucks carrying police and soldiers armed with antiriot weapons and fire trucks with water hoses and other gear. The fire trucks trained their powerful hoses on the students, and the police and soldiers advanced on the leaders with clubs and tear gas. The march was broken up, and the other leaders and I were arrested and taken to prison.

The penitentiary was a large, primitive, frightening building on the outskirts of São Paulo. It was surrounded by a high wall, the top of which was covered with metal spikes. Its interior was like that of any other prison. When the police trucks arrived there, all the students were lined up to be registered and fingerprinted, accompanied by a lot of kicking and beating. Having completed the legal formalities, the police then assigned two students to each cell. My cellmate happened to be one of my classmates at the night school, which made life there slightly more bearable. But the prison was foul. Large rats, roaches, and other creatures ran about in the intense heat and filth. Toilet facilities were collective. There was no open area where prisoners could take exercise or get some fresh air.

I spent the first night in the jail not thinking of my situation and its consequences for my educational plans, but worrying about the effects of this affair on my family, and particularly my mother. Frankly, I feared facing my mother's anger more than I feared the police. The next morning we were interrogated again, and in the process we were kicked and beaten by the special investigative agents of the federal government. They wanted to know who was behind our movement and strongly suspected Communist agents. We could not convince them that our revolt was spontaneous, directed against the suppression of freedom.

After two days in prison, I was surprised and in despair that no one from my family had come to visit. To be sure, I was not eager to see them gloat over the failure of my educational plans, but even so I was upset. Then I learned that no parents had come to visit, that in fact they waited outside the prison walls every day but were not allowed any contact with us. I also learned that my mother was having fits every day about my being in prison instead of in the store making money. She had appealed to influential Lebanese to intercede with the government on my behalf. She found a distant relative, named Alfredo, in the government and begged him to help get me released. This young man later had a most important influence on my future.

After one month of interrogations, beatings, deprivations, and humiliations, the police concluded that our revolt had indeed been spontaneous and not Communist-inspired. So we were all released by order of the supreme dictator and allowed to return to school.

I took the streetcar from the prison gate straight home. All during the ride I prepared myself to face my mother. I dreaded the moment. Finally I walked in the door, filthy and smelling; I had not taken a bath or changed clothes in a month. My mother was at the top of the stairway. I got exactly what I expected.

The following day I returned to my routine, working during the day and studying at night.

8 · *The Struggle to Become a Doctor*

WHEN my Uncle George left with his wife and daughter to visit the United States and Canada, he planned to stay three or four months and he leased his house to us. However, shortly after his arrival in western Canada, his wife became seriously ill, and he wrote us that they would not be able to return for nine months or a year.

On hearing this news, my mother called a family meeting and announced: "We cannot remain employees at a fixed salary all our life. We should buy the store from Uncle George when he comes back." My oldest brother pointed out that we did not have enough money to make a down payment. "That's no problem," my mother yelled. "You'll never get anywhere if you don't learn to scheme!" She then outlined her plot. First, Mussa was to fire the two employees who were faithful to Uncle George and replace them with my two younger brothers, who were to leave school and get to work. Second, I was to remain as the main cashier and see to it that the books showed very little profit when my uncle returned. Third, she persuaded my grandmother to take our side when we negotiated with George.

George's wife died, and George and his daughter, Yvonne, returned to São Paulo after an absence of about a year. Yvonne was heartbroken about her mother's death and about leaving her buried in distant western

Canada. Luckily for us, she refused to return to the house where she and her mother had lived, so her father bought a new house. Thus we were left in the old house, for which, of course, we had to pay rent.

George spent the first four weeks settling his daughter in the new house and taking care of the legal matters resulting from his wife's death. In the fifth week, he asked me to show him the store's books. My oldest brother, the manager, was present. George was shocked and angry to see the meager profit made during his absence. The poor profit, along with my inability to collect his promissory notes, made him lose faith in me as a businessman altogether.

Also, he was surprised that virtually all the old employees had left and that all of us were working in the store. Mussa explained that such a move was necessary to save money: the other employees' salaries had been too high and they had asked for a raise. But Uncle George was shrewd, and he immediately became suspicious.

That same day my mother asked him to dinner to discuss some matters of importance. After dinner, in the presence of all of us, including my grandmother, my mother said formally: "George, you should sell the store to your nephews. We're a big family now and we can't live forever on salaries." George protested that he intended to go on managing the store. That statement was followed by one of my mother's famous explosions. She reminded him that my father had saved him, George, and the rest of the family from starvation and disease. "Who urged you to come to Brazil?" she shouted. "Who paid for your ticket? Who taught you how to be a man? Eh?"

Few people ever resisted my mother's demands. George was no exception. That evening he signed a document promising to transfer the store to us after agreement on financial terms. A few days later we made a token initial payment, and the rest was provided for by promissory notes, which were due over a ten-year period.

Two months after George returned, the store was ours. My brothers quickly tripled its size and also opened several branches throughout the city. Then they started their own clothing factory, to supply the retail stores. Naturally my mother was the driving force behind all this.

I continued working in the store in the daytime and studying at night until the end of 1935. I saved as much money as I could. In addition, when we bought the store from George, we turned it into a private corporation, and each one of us had shares in proportion to his years of service.

I knew that 1936 would be a crucial year for me for two reasons. First, all the subjects required for admission to the university would be concentrated in that year. In Brazil at that time, one could not major in one subject or take electives. Whether one wanted to become a doctor, an engineer, or a lawyer, in that final year one had to take all the required subjects. Furthermore, the university entrance exam was given only three months after final exams at the night school.

Second, I decided to compete for admission to the State University of São Paulo. Admission to the private medical school in São Paulo was easy, but I could not possibly afford the tuition. Besides, the State University Medical School had an excellent reputation, and seventy students were selected on a fellowship basis every year from about 1,000 candidates, through one of the toughest and most unbiased competitive examinations anywhere. To avoid pressure from relatives with influence, the examiners were brought from other cities, and their names were kept secret up to the last minute. The entrance competition consisted of written and oral examinations in physiology, zoology, chemistry (organic and biological), physics, mathematics, sociology, philosophy, and theology.

Faced with the enormous academic challenge, I decided to stop working in the store and concentrate on my studies. I first approached my oldest brother, who was now the head of the firm, and told him of my intention to sell my shares in the business and use the money to support myself. He had no objection. However, he said that he could not buy my shares in cash, because they were short of funds, and instead he would give me promissory notes that would be due every three months. I decided to postpone my decision on this matter until later.

The next major obstacle was my mother. I went to see her just after New Year's. As expected, I got a tremendous barrage of recrimination: "Now that the business is starting to boom you are on the way to the poorhouse!" She tried to make me change my mind and mobilized relatives and friends to do the same. When all her efforts failed, she said: "Go ahead and do what you want. But you'll be back in the store in less than a year, and I'll see to it personally that you start again at the bottom." This was one of the few times she was ever wrong.

I received my last salary from the store on January 30, 1936. I thought the savings that I had accumulated would be sufficient to carry me through until I got into medical school. I paid my mother a monthly amount for my room and board, so that I would not be a burden to anyone. I then set up the following daily routine: 7:00 to 9:00 A.M.: reading in bed after breakfast; 9:30 to 11:30 A.M.: studying in the main public library; 12:00 noon: light lunch at home; 1:00 to 5:00 P.M.: studying and doing schoolwork at home. I would then have something to eat and by 6:30 P.M. would be at the night school. After school was over at 10:00, I would join my friends and go back to our hot arguments next door to the chicken coop until 1:00 A.M., when I took the last streetcar home.

When the end of the school year arrived, we took the final exams. I passed with an average of ninety-eight, as did my three friends. We celebrated by getting drunk in a good restaurant. We each planned to pursue a different course of study at the university, but we agreed to meet again after the entrance examinations.

I told my family about my first academic success. No one was impressed. My mother still thought that I was wasting my time, that sooner or later, after my savings were exhausted, I would return to the store.

I now concentrated all my energies on getting accepted into medical school. I asked my mother to bring my lunch and dinner to my room. I did not want to see anyone. I worked and studied and filled page after page with notes. Being blessed with a phenomenal memory, I was able to store away an enormous amount of data. It was a crusade not only to accomplish my own goal and satisfy my ego, but also to conquer my family's opposition, and particularly my mother's. I remained in my room for three months.

The exams were held in a large garagelike hall in the basement of the medical school and in several large lecture halls in the main building. There were close to nine hundred candidates, mostly native Brazilians from wealthy families. Each student was thoroughly searched for hidden notes and assigned a desk for the written examinations, which lasted six days. These were followed by oral examinations, twelve in all, each lasting an hour, covering a three-week period. There followed two months of nerve-racking waiting for the results, until one day the news spread rapidly that the list of those who had gained admission to medical school had been posted outside the office of the school secretary. I could not decide whether to rush to school by taxicab or travel slowly by streetcar, so afraid was I to look at the list and not see my name.

A huge crowd stood in line to see the list. Upon getting close, some jumped with joy; others walked away head down, almost in tears. Suddenly I spotted my name, the third from the top, the third-highest average among the nine hundred candidates.

I walked back to the streetcar barely touching the ground. The world was mine. I said nothing to my family until dinnertime. When I did, my oldest brother smiled; my mother complained again, saying that it was a waste and that I would be back in the store in no time.

The school year was not to start for two months, so for the first time in my life I took a week's vacation. I went to a health resort outside São Paulo to rest and sleep, and returned home recharged and ready to go, my life planned for the next six years.

9 · *Medical School*

THE first three years of medical school were largely devoted to basic sciences: anatomy, physiology, pathology, histology, pharmacology, and biochemistry. For detailed dissections of the human body, we had an abundance of cadavers, and I became proficient in anatomical dissection, particularly of the nervous system. I was soon appointed teaching assistant and was given the keys to the anatomy laboratory so that at night I could prepare the cadavers for the following day's lectures.

But an economic problem nagged me from the very first day in medical school. My savings had dwindled rapidly; six months after I started, there was nothing left. I asked my brothers for a loan on my share in the business, but they said that they were short of cash and that business was bad. Therefore I decided to look for a part-time job. But what kind of job would give me a sufficient income and at the same time allow me to pursue my heavy academic curriculum? I sought advice from my professors in the basic sciences. The chairman of the Anatomy Department found three wealthy students for me to tutor, but what they paid was hardly enough to cover the cost of meals. I also tutored several others in physiology, which was, and continued to be, my favorite subject.

My professor of pharmacology told me that a number

of pharmaceutical companies employed medical students as detail men to promote their drugs with doctors in practice. He gave me the names of several drug companies, among them Silva Araujo-Roussell, the firm formed through the merger of a Brazilian concern and a French drug manufacturer.

I presented myself to the medical director of Silva Araujo-Roussell, Dr. Abram Ackerman. He was a brilliant neurologist, trained in France at the famous neurology clinic of Jean Martin Charcot. Although he was respected and consulted by every neurologist in São Paulo and Rio, he was unable to obtain a license to practice medicine in Brazil. Dr. Ackerman and his wife, Mina, who was in charge of advertising and promotion, explained to me that the company's policy was to employ only full-time people. I told them that as a medical student I would have easier access to doctors and could accomplish as much as, if not more than, a full-time salesman. Finally I said: "Please try me for a month. If you aren't satisfied, I'll leave without any payment."

Both Ackerman and his wife were impressed by the sincerity of my plea and decided to consult the company's president in Rio de Janeiro. Three days later, Ackerman told me I had the job. "I convinced the president that we should have a permanent man in the university hospital," he said. "You are going to be that man. Work hard and show the company that their faith in you is justified."

Two days later I started as a detail man for Silva Araujo-Roussell Laboratories at a salary that was twice what I had been making in the store. During the first week I accompanied another detail man to learn the trade; after that I was on my own. First, I asked Ackerman to assign me three to four specific drugs for promotion, so that he would have a yardstick by which to measure my efficiency. Second, I studied the drugs thoroughly and made a list of the names of the major and most reputed specialists who might use them. Third, I called on each one of them and told them about the drugs and my situation. Within three months I tripled sales.

My accomplishment in such a short period of time brought me tremendous prestige, not only with Ackerman and his wife, but also with all the important company officers. Within a year I was considered one of the best detail men and was promptly promoted. I entered competitions and won prizes offered by the company for promotional ideas for new drugs. Within two years I was appointed assistant to the medical director and my salary increased considerably. I was able not only to defray a large share of the expenses at home, but also to assist my brothers in expanding their business. This progress continued yearly until I finished my medical studies and graduated.

The first three years of medical school passed rapidly. The entire school, including its administrative organization and departmental structure, was modeled on French and German universities. The chairman of each department was considered by everyone to be the sole and absolute ruler; he was the only one addressed as "Professor." The teachers who assisted him were at his mercy and could be dismissed without explanation. They resembled the vassals or courtiers of a king. The professor's contact with the students was rare. Although the class was small, he hardly knew anyone's name. He would give a theoretical lecture every week or two, entering the classroom only after everyone had been seated. His assistants answered questions. This system was prevalent in both the basic sciences and the clinical departments.

At the end of the third year there was a tough final exam in each subject. In physiology I passed at the top of the class, as I had in all the exams throughout the three years. I also placed among the top ten in anatomy, biochemistry, and pharmacology. In the morphological sciences, however, which required sitting down and looking at slides of dead tissues through a microscope, I was weak. My restless nature was not suitable for microscopic studies. Consequently, I almost failed the final exam in pathology and barely passed the one in histology. Looking back, I think the instructors in those two subjects let me pass only because they knew I was working hard to earn a living.

With the beginning of the fourth year of medical school, the instruction shifted almost entirely to the hospital of Santa Casa, which was the city hospital. At that time the university did not have a hospital of its own. Internal medicine, surgery, gynecology, radiology, ophthalmology, neurology, and neurosurgery were taught in Santa Casa. Obstetrics, pediatrics, and public health were taught in other buildings in the vicinity of the medical school.

With the move to Santa Casa and the beginning of clinical teaching, my double life as a student and a drug-company employee became considerably simpler. It was now easy for me to persuade the professors and their assistants to order my drugs through the hospital pharmacy and to prescribe them in the outpatient departments. Consequently, my drug sales zoomed.

The clinical curriculum of all Brazilian medical schools was extremely complex and full of duplication. There were three departments of internal medicine and one of infectious diseases, each having an independent chairman with a retinue of assistants. Surgery had three or four departments, and gynecology was separate from obstetrics. These many divisions were in contrast to American medical schools, where there was usually one department of medicine and one of surgery. The multiplication of departments led to considerable redundancies in teaching, as well as to friction and rivalries among the heads of the various sections and their staffs. The students were caught in the middle.

The first year in the clinical departments was devoted to propaedeutics and clinical diagnosis in both internal medicine and surgery. The emphasis was on how to use the patient's personal and family history to make an accurate assessment of the signs and symptoms, and how to perform a thorough physical examination. Radiography and laboratory tests were to be requested only when absolutely necessary and were subsidiary to the information obtained by clinical examination. This procedure contrasts with today's approach in clinical medicine, where hundreds of laboratory tests and radiological examinations are carried out on a given case before the doctor even sees the patient.

I spent one year in internal medicine, rotating through the various departments. Although it was a fruitful and interesting period, I did not opt for internal medicine as a specialty. We dealt mostly with old people and patients debilitated by tuberculosis, malaria, terminal malignancy, or nervous-system diseases, usually secondary to syphilis. In Brazil at that time, patients so afflicted came to that hospital only in the advanced stages of their diseases. They presented a challenge in terms of clinical diagnosis and attempted management, but the outcome was usually predictable: death and final verification in the autopsy room.

I passed all the exams in internal medicine, but in the one for infectious diseases I had a frightening experience. The examiner, the chairman of the department, was fond of me and was aware that I was clumsy with the microscope. He asked me to examine a slide made from the blood of a man with an infectious disease and to diagnose the organism. He handed me the slide upside down, and for over thirty minutes I struggled to get the blood smear in focus, taking care not to crack the slide. After seeing my utter frustration, he asked me to turn the slide over. Only then did I realize that he was playing a trick on me. Fortunately, I was then able to make the diagnosis, and he gave me a high grade.

I spent the following year rotating in the various surgical services. There the emphasis was primarily on manual skill. The prestige that a surgeon enjoyed among assistants, staff, and students was based on how fast he could remove a stomach or spleen or perform any other surgical feat from "skin to skin"—that is, from the time of the incision to the time of skin closure.

I was not greatly impressed by the surgical specialty or the personal attitude of the surgeons. I gathered throughout the year that in order to be a surgeon, one had to have a kind of personality I did not have. Therefore I ruled out surgery as my specialty. Since I had not as yet been exposed to any other clinical discipline, such as obstetrics or gynecology, I decided not to make up my mind about a given field of specialization until the last year of medical school. I had heard a great deal about how fascinating the field of obstetrics was and wanted to check those rumors myself.

Meanwhile, although my time could have been totally absorbed by my work for the drug company and by my studies, I could not keep away from politics. Probably because of my background, international politics has always fascinated me. No matter how busy I was at that time, or am today, I feel intellectually and emotionally involved in international problems.

During the invasion of Ethiopia by Mussolini, our class was divided. Students of Italian origin sided with Mussolini, while the others, including me, were for the Ethiopian underdogs. Headed at that time by the dictator Vargas, the Brazilian government wholeheartedly supported both Mussolini and Hitler. Despite the attitude of the Brazilian government and the restrictions it imposed on overt antagonism toward Mussolini's adventures, I was able to gather a small group of students sympathetic to the Ethiopians. We collected signatures on petitions and sent telegrams to the representatives of England and France in the League of Nations, asking them to give full moral, economic, and military support to the Ethiopians. When Ethiopia was finally defeated, we tore the Italian flag to pieces in the streets and fought with the fascists.

Similarly, during the Spanish Civil War my heart was with the Republicans. My group hated Franco and his "foreign legions." We collected medical supplies for the Republican armies, but the government would not permit us to ship them. When the Germans destroyed Guernica, we declared a day of mourning and refused to attend classes. When Toledo and Madrid fell, and Franco became the absolute ruler of Spain, our hearts were broken. We despaired that democratic nations would ever be able to oppose totalitarian regimes.

Such feelings were soon confirmed when Hitler began crushing one neighboring nation after another. My liberal colleagues and I watched with great horror the abject and humiliating pilgrimage of Chamberlain, Daladier, and their cohorts to Munich. With great sadness we learned of their capitulations to Hitler's demands and their betrayal of Austria, Czechoslovakia, and Poland. There was no doubt in our minds that the second holocaust of this century would soon engulf the nations of the world.

When war was finally declared, none of us was surprised. But what was shocking and agonizing was the rapid and crushing defeat of France and the lack of preparedness of the English armies. To compound our misery, Vargas gave moral support and promised material assistance to Hitler and Mussolini. At that time I did not have too much love or respect for France, but I had considerably less for the totalitarian regimes of Germany and Italy. Although I had then, and still have, great respect and admiration for the British system of parliamentary government, I was utterly disheartened by that country's repeated surrender to Hitler's demands.

Nevertheless, and despite my ambiguous feelings, my sympathy was with the Allies. My liberal friends met at the home of one of our wealthy colleagues. We pasted large maps of the world on the walls and used pins with heads of different colors to designate the positions of the various armies. Arguments and fights arose between us and those who were on the side of the dictators.

When the United States finally entered the war, and President Roosevelt convinced Vargas to drop his support for the dictators, the whole Brazilian nation threw its support to the Allies. A Brazilian expeditionary force was formed to fight on the side of the Allied armies in Italy. We cheered those of our professors and colleagues who volunteered to go with this force.

Brazil celebrated the Allied victories, first in Europe and then in the Pacific, with more enthusiasm and noise than the Americans in the United States. That's how Latins are.

10 · First Love

IN the middle of this turbulent life of working for the drug company, keeping up with my difficult academic curriculum, and involving myself with the politics of World War II, I fell in love for the first time.

Latin males are usually obsessed with sexual adventures and extremely proud of their conquests, and Brazilians are no exception. Throughout the years I spent in Brazil, I felt at a great disadvantage with my friends when sex was discussed. My struggles for survival in Lebanon and my busy schedule since then had left me little time for romance.

One night in the women's surgical ward, a patient was admitted with sharp abdominal pain. I diagnosed it as acute appendicitis and called the assistant professor to perform the emergency surgery. I also summoned Carina, the surgical nurse on call, who had occasionally helped me examine patients. Carina was extremely attractive, tanned, blond, blue-eyed, and somewhat older than I. She came from a wealthy family and worked as a volunteer. Every time we met alone in the corridors or in the wards, she would give me a sweet, encouraging smile, but I was too busy to respond.

The assistant professor arrived promptly, followed by Carina. She prepared the operating room, and we three proceeded with the surgery. I stood opposite the surgeon, and Carina stood next to me, passing the instruments. Each time Carina's leg accidentally touched mine I shivered slightly. The operation was simple; the inflamed appendix was removed, and the surgeon asked me to close the skin and return the patient to the ward. Afterward Carina and I went to the canteen to have a cup of coffee.

Sitting across from each other at the table, we talked about medicine, poverty, and war, about totalitarianism versus democracy, about literature. I looked at my watch. It was past midnight. I had to stay in the hospital because I was on call through the night, but we made a date for dinner on the following evening.

We met in a small Italian restaurant in the downtown area and enjoyed a delightful and relaxing meal. At first our conversation continued along the lines of the night before, but then she asked me to tell her about my life. I gave her a full account of my past history in Lebanon, including the death of my father, the ordeal in the French camp, the trip to Brazil, and my struggle with my family because I wanted to become a doctor. Her eyes were moist and she took my hand and pressed it warmly.

It was my turn to ask her about her life. She did not hesitate. She was almost thirty-two, she said. Her parents were Italian. They had left Italy because they abhorred fascism. Her father was a wealthy man, a Renaissance scholar, poet, and writer; her mother was a housewife. Carina had a sister; both lived with their parents, both had received an excellent education and were raised in a highly intellectual environment.

At twenty-three Carina had met a man slightly older than she, the manager of a famous restaurant in São Paulo. They fell madly in love and got married. In education and cultural background, there was a wide difference between them; he had never completed high school and was not interested in books or culture. Nevertheless, she tried hard not to let this difference disturb their marriage. Shortly after the birth of their son, her husband's behavior changed completely. He would leave home for two or three days without any explanation. He lost all interest in his family and had no affection for the boy.

Carina sought the help of friends and a psychiatrist, but that made her husband worse than ever. They constantly argued, and he beat her badly. In fact, he became so vicious that she carried a gun to protect herself and the child.

One day she went away for a weekend with her parents, taking the boy with her. When she returned home, she found her husband in their own bed with a prostitute. She shot him in the abdomen. She immediately called for an ambulance and surrendered to the police, entrusting the care of her boy to her family. Her husband recovered completely and within a few months was back at work. Carina went to jail.

Her father had hired the best lawyers for her defense. In Brazil then there was no jury system; a judge or group of judges decided a case. At the trial Carina was allowed to speak in her own defense, and her speech to the court was one of the most brilliant emotional defenses of its time. She was sentenced to three years in a minimum-security prison.

One of her lawyers fell wildly in love with her. He convinced the prison authorities to let Carina work in the library and teach other women prisoners. He proposed to her, but she refused him. Carina put all her heart and energy into the education of women inmates, taught them how to read and write, solicited donations of money and books, and created a fine library.

In less than two years she was released because of her excellent behavior and humanitarian work toward rehabilitating other prisoners. After her release she still went to the prison three times a week on a volunteer basis to take care of the library she had organized and to continue her rehabilitation work.

Some two years before the beginning of World War II, her father decided to visit Italy, which he knew so well and loved. He took Carina and her son along. They spent six months touring museums and libraries, listening to music and opera, and visiting churches. Following their return to Brazil, Carina worked at various jobs until finally she decided on nursing.

When she had finished telling me her story, a sadness descended on us both and we felt a great warmth for each other. There was a bond between us that went beyond friendship, created by the turbulence we had both experienced in our lives.

We left the restaurant hand in hand and walked along the busy downtown streets. We came to a small hotel used by one-night lovers. Without ceremony or persuasion, we walked in, rented a room, and spent the night in each other's arms. We made love several times and slept soundly in the certainty that our affair would last a long time.

Carina's sister had a lovely apartment near the downtown area. Carina arranged with her for us to use the apartment when she was at work or out of town. We met there whenever we could. After lovemaking, Carina read to me from Dante, Erasmus, Comte, Shakespeare. She also recited poetry, for she had a fabulous memory, and she danced in imitation of Isadora Duncan, for whom she had great admiration. She was vastly more cultured than I, and I gladly accepted her tutoring. With occasional interruptions, our meetings continued until I finished medical school and left Brazil for the United States.

Carina's moral support and encouragement were invaluable to me during my struggle with my family and during periods of depression that hit me in severe crises. But her assistance and unselfishness reached their height after I finished my medical education and could not decide what to do. She offered to secure a loan for me from her father to help me open an office, but I refused. Although she was a great source of strength and on occasion assisted me financially, she never mentioned the word *marriage*.

Before I got involved with Carina, I had been seeing a girl named Helena. My relationship with her was pure infatuation; we had nothing in common at all. We met somewhere, made love, and then ignored each other until our next meeting. Two months after we had once met this way, she told me she was pregnant. We decided to go through a marriage ceremony performed by a priest, even though neither she nor I wanted to be tied up in a marriage.

On July 25, 1942, a beautiful boy was born. We named him Nicolau Ruben Araujo Assali. Two months after his birth, our religious marriage was annulled. Later, when he joined me in Cincinnati and became an American citizen, he changed his name to Robin.

11 · Graduation and First Practice

THE sixth and final year of medical school was largely devoted to obstetrics and gynecology. I was not interested in my minor courses—ophthalmology, radiology, public health, and forensic medicine—but studied enough to pass the exams.

With obstetrics it was a different story. This discipline appealed to me from the start, for several reasons. First, it dealt with young people who came to the hospital to have a healthy experience and were rewarded with a new life. Second, obstetrics presented some of the most exciting challenges in medicine; when obstetrical complications occur, they require skill and knowledge in all fields of medicine. Third, of all the medical specialties, obstetrics at that time offered the widest range for innovative ideas and imaginative research; the specialty had long been practiced by midwives and conservative physicians unreceptive to new approaches. Finally, there was a personal element as well. I met a young assistant professor by the name of Domingos Delascio, a dynamic and stimulating teacher. He was working hard to move up the academic ladder through what in Brazil they called a "docente livre"—a major competition, entailing the preparation of an original thesis as well as a number of written, oral, and practical exams. Delascio invited me to join a small team of students who met one night a week at his home to help him prepare his thesis.

My association with Delascio lasted until I left Brazil. We worked together with his obstetrical and gynecological patients. He also taught me how to write scientific papers for medical journals; we were co-authors of three papers reporting unusual cases.

In reviewing obstetrical complications, we argued heatedly about a particular disease called "toxemia of pregnancy." It was referred to as "the obstetrical enigma and the disease of theories." We asked ourselves why young women should suffer high blood pressure, protein in the urine, swelling, and convulsions ending in death. Delascio would say, "This is an area where a man could make a major contribution"—a sentence that was implanted in my mind forever.

Oddly enough, I almost flunked the final exam in obstetrics—the subject that I most liked—and for a very unusual reason. I had passed the written test with a high grade. For the oral I was examined by the chairman of the Obstetrics Department, who was also a scholar in the Portuguese language and a member of the National Academy of Letters. He asked me to describe the method of performing a breech delivery. I answered accurately, but in the process used a Portuguese word that he considered vulgar. He gave me hell in front of the other students for defiling the beautiful Portuguese language. I tried to explain that I was a foreigner, but to no avail. He ordered me to study Portuguese for three months and return for a second trial. When I returned, I was, fortunately, examined by one of the assistants, who did not care as much for the Portuguese language. I passed easily.

The last three months of medical school were almost entirely devoted to the graduation ceremonies. In Brazil, graduation from the university was a big event. On the eve of the ceremony there was a banquet. Speech after speech was made, the students thanking the professors, the professors thanking the students.

The graduation ceremony was held at the Municipal Theater at 8:00 P.M. It was attended by students, professors, parents, and numerous civil and military dignitaries. The ceremony began with the singing of the national anthem, followed by a prayer and a short speech by the rector of the university, after which the university officials called out the names of the students in alphabetical order. Each student received his diploma amid applause, shook hands with the officials, and returned to his seat. My mother, my sister, all my brothers, and a few other relatives attended. For the first time in six years they acknowledged my effort. That night, at least, they were proud of me. Also present in the audience, and representing the governor of the state of São Paulo, was my distant cousin Alfredo Issa Assali (in Brazil the name was spelled *Assaly*). He had risen through the government ranks to become the equivalent of a state attorney general in the United States, a very important position in Brazil. He was pleased to see one of his relatives, whom he had rescued from prison a few years before, among those graduating with honors.

Although I was the chairman of the committee that put together the graduating-class speech, because of my heavy accent the speech was delivered by a close friend and colleague. The theme was "Medicine and War": the contrast between the destruction of war and the healing of medicine, and the paradox that war and medicine benefit from each other. The speech was received with a standing ovation and the ceremony ended with each new doctor being hugged, kissed, and congratulated by relatives and friends. Carina was there, too, full of pride.

It was past midnight when I got home, still in my academic robes and clutching my diploma, wide awake with excitement. I finally fell asleep and didn't get up until noon.

The next day I felt terribly let down and just as confused as I had been when I was released from the French camp in Lebanon. Now what was I to do? I had resigned from the drug company six months before graduation. The company wanted me to stay; they had offered me an attractive promotion, but I wanted to become a practicing doctor, not a doctor working for a drug company.

I did not have money to establish my own practice. Moreover, at that time very few doctors in Brazil took on partners. I was in near despair when two weeks later Delascio offered me a job. When he outlined the details however, I turned him down politely and told him that I preferred to continue studying with him and assisting him on an informal basis. Carina made new suggestions every day. She wanted me to accept her money; she wanted me to use her sister's apartment without rent, and she would work as my nurse and secretary. I turned down all these offers because, I guess, I was proud.

My family sensed my unhappiness. Only my blunt mother finally asked what I planned to do next. I said I did not know. She told me to go back to the store: "You'll make ten times more money than you would as a doctor."

I walked out of the house one day determined to find my own solution. I took a streetcar downtown, got off in the main square, and decided to have a drink in a nearby bar. This was unusual, because, as a matter of principle, I never drank during the day. I left the bar and strolled over to a street where many doctors' offices were located. Suddenly someone tapped my shoulder. It was a general practitioner I had called on when I worked for the drug company. His busy practice included some gynecological surgery and obstetrics as well. He invited me up to his office.

We chatted briefly, and then he asked, simply: "Why don't you join me in my practice? I have a lot of obstetrical and gynecological cases that I can't handle, but you could." He proposed that I keep seventy-five percent of all I made from the patients I handled. The remaining twenty-five percent would cover my share of the office expenses. A couple of days later I decided to give it a trial. It was easily the best offer I had had. As I understood it, I would be deciding on the management of the obstetrical and gynecological cases. Also, I was to hang my diploma on the wall and have my name at the main entrance. But I was in no hurry to do this. Something held me back.

Hardly had I settled in the new office when the doctor called me to examine a patient with slight vaginal bleeding. He had already taken her history, performed the physical examination, and made a diagnosis. He only wanted my approval to do the surgery.

He introduced me to the patient as a great specialist who had just joined his practice. I asked the patient a few basic questions. She told me that the good doctor, my partner—or boss, if you will—had been giving her shots of estrogen three times a week for the last three months. I performed a pelvic examination and found nothing wrong. While the patient dressed, the doctor and I retreated to his office. "A nice hysterectomy I got for you as your first case," he said. I was shocked. "But this patient doesn't need a hysterectomy," I said. "She is young and her uterus is normal. We just have to stop the hormone treatment. Why are you giving her estrogen, anyway?" I asked.

He turned pale as he shot back, "But I told the patient

she must have her uterus removed. You can't contradict me." I answered, "I'm sorry. I won't operate. It would be a crime. It's an unnecessary operation, and one with a high mortality rate." He told me to go back to my office, that he would take care of the problem. Later I learned that he referred the case to another surgeon; he assisted in the operation, and they split the fee.

I sat in my office bewildered by the experience. Though my forebodings about the association had been realized, I decided to give my partner the benefit of the doubt. For the next two days I did not see him. His male nurse told me that the doctor had gone to his farm to attend to some problems. The nurse was taking care of the old patients who came for their shots; the new ones were given appointments for some other time. I saw no one during that period.

When he returned to the office, the doctor was very friendly. He said he had followed my advice and told the patient she did not need to have her uterus removed. During the next couple of weeks he referred a few patients to me with minor problems. I gave them medication and instructions and told them not to return unless they had new complications. Meanwhile, my colleague did not ask me to see any major gynecological or obstetrical cases, nor did he refer any to me.

One day he walked into my office and gave me a lecture on medicine and economics. "You're sending all these patients away after giving them a prescription," he said. "That's no way to practice medicine; we can't pay the rent if we do that. You have to keep them coming by giving them shots or some kind of treatment here in the office."

I was stunned. Finally, I regained my composure. "This is not the way I intend to practice medicine. You should look for another partner," I told him.

"You'll starve if you practice medicine your way," he mumbled.

One week later I said good-bye and never saw him or set foot in his office again.

Once more I was unemployed. I felt that my family's opposition to my studying medicine might have been justified. Without my diploma and without the label "doctor," it would have been easy to find all kinds of jobs. But the pride that diploma gave me, coupled with my hatred of admitting defeat—particularly to my mother—prevented me from looking for anything else. I was determined to be a doctor. And my family did not ask me to pay for room and board, I still had some savings in the bank, and Carina was helping.

One day I went back to the medical school and discussed my problem with the chairman of the Department of Physiology. He welcomed me warmly and asked if I would be willing to work as an instructor but without any official academic title. He promised some small remuneration. I accepted his offer and started work the same day.

I was happy to get back to physiology, my favorite subject, and basic research again, even though I did not have an official position or financial rewards. To keep my hand in clinical medicine, I also worked as a volunteer without pay in the city Polyclinic, a sort of outpatient department for the poor.

After only three months in the Physiology Department I had a lucky break: exposure to a new aspect of medicine that taught me a valuable lesson about human behavior.

12 · Two Years Among the Girls

IN those days prostitutes in São Paulo were divided into two categories. One consisted of those who operated through private contacts in expensive apartments maintained by executives of big corporations or by rich individuals. They were not registered or controlled by any government authority and were known as the "hidden" or "underground" or "illegal" prostitutes. And there were those who served the population at large and were quartered in an official red-light district known as the *Zona* in Portuguese. The Zone comprised some six or seven interconnected streets lined on both sides by buildings of different sizes and varying degrees of neatness. Some were little more than slum buildings and housed the cheapest girls; others were in better condition and housed the more expensive girls.

Each house, regardless of price, had one main entrance with the upper half of the door replaced by a grille. Some houses also had front windows covered by grilles. By law, the girls were to remain inside the houses at night and make their inducements from behind the grilles. Nevertheless, the more expensive houses, with the acquiescence of the bribed police, permitted their girls to go outside to solicit customers.

The houses were ruled with an iron hand by a group of madams. Each had a territory of her own, consisting of one or two houses, depending on the size of the houses and the number of girls. They reported their activities to the underworld bosses, who collected every penny the girls made. The bulk of the income was withheld for "expenses and maintenance," which made the girls total slaves, dependent for their subsistence entirely on the house for as long as they could function as sex machines.

The Zone was constantly patrolled by police, particularly on weekend nights when the streets were jammed with men looking through the grilled doors. Fights often broke out both inside and outside the houses, but the police seldom made any arrests.

In co-operation with the Department of Public Security, the city Health Department maintained an outpatient clinic where the prostitutes had checkups for venereal disease. The clinic was located next to the Zone and was staffed by three full-time doctors and a dozen nurses. The number of legally registered prostitutes in the Zone was about six hundred, but the actual number was larger.

About six months after my graduation, while working in physiology and at the same time looking desperately for a job with a salary, I got a call from my cousin Alfredo. He was now the head of the Department of Public Security, which supervised the police, the prisons, the secret investigative apparatus of the state, and the legal prostitution division. Alfredo welcomed me to his office and offered me the job as head of the clinic of the legal prostitution division. We discussed at length the duties involved and the degree of freedom I would have in imposing health regulations. He was somewhat vague on this, mainly because he did not know the nature of the problems involved. When he pointed out that the job offered great possibilities for research, I accepted promptly.

Two days later I reported to the clinic as its head and called a meeting of the staff to familiarize myself with the organization and functioning of the service. Although the law required each girl to have one checkup a week, very few conformed. There was no satisfactory explanation as to why the law was not enforced.

One thing was clear to me immediately: the clinic was understaffed. I appealed to my cousin for additional funds to hire more people, but all he was able to give me was enough money for one part-time physician and two nurses. It was better than nothing. Carina joined me, as a volunteer.

It did not take long to get to the bottom of the weekly examination problem. The tip-off came from a young woman whom I found infected with gonorrhea and chancroid. I told her not to have sexual intercourse and to return in three days. She laughed. "The madam won't let me stop working. And she'll never let me come back here." I decided to tackle the problem directly. I called the head of the police division in charge of the Zone and asked him to summon all the madams to a meeting with me on a given date. I explained to him why I wanted this meeting. He tried hard to discourage me from such a venture, but when he saw that I was determined, he promised to do exactly as I asked. He knew I had the backing of my cousin, who was his boss.

On the appointed day and hour, more than fifty madams gathered in the waiting room. And a strange gathering it was—a galaxy of colors, shapes, ages, thin and fat, all wearing heavy makeup, and lots of jewelry on arms, necks, and ears.

I proceeded to point out the importance of the checkups, not only for their girls, but also for the population as a whole. I demonstrated statistically that prompt treatment would eradicate venereal disease from the

Zone in a short time. I got carried away: "With the diseases under control, more customers will come and business will boom."

They seemed pleased at the prospect. Then I came to the critical point. "It's only fair to let you know," I said after a pause, "that from now on every girl with venereal disease will be isolated. She will not be permitted to do any of her usual work until she is pronounced cured. I will ask the authorities to close any house that violates this rule until full compliance is obtained."

Pandemonium broke out after my last words. Obscene shouts echoed from all sides. Threats were hurled with abandon. But I was calm and closed the meeting with a simple statement that I expected the girls with appointments for the next day to keep them.

My work with the prostitutes began in earnest the day after the meeting with the madams and lasted for two years. During the first few weeks, the clinic functioned fairly well. The girls came for checkups at regular intervals. Those with gonorrhea were promptly treated with sulfa drugs. Penicillin, however, was still scarce and hard to get. Treating syphilis continued to be a problem, and I was not satisfied with our ability to impose isolation on the infected girls.

Soon I decided to visit some of the houses in the Zone to observe the living conditions and routines of the girls. In particular, I wanted to make sure that the infected girls whom I had instructed not to "work" did not "work." To prevent the madams from preparing a show for me, I decided to make a surprise visit. I did not alert the police either.

I did have to clear the plan with Alfredo, who was the highest authority in this matter. I told him that unless we improved hygienic conditions at the source and unless our isolation system was strictly followed, there was little hope of stemming the tide of venereal diseases. I was certain the madams were sabotaging our efforts and were not paying any attention to our regulations. Alfredo approved in principle the idea of visiting the houses but insisted that a police officer accompany me. I told him that I preferred to do it alone because I did not trust the officers in charge of patrolling the Zone. "Most of them are on the payroll of the madams and their bosses," I said.

"Nick, you are making a serious accusation against the police department. They are under my jurisdiction. Do you have any proof?" he asked.

"No, I don't have any proof but I am certain of it anyway; everything I have confided to the officers in the past few weeks has been repeated to me by the madams," I replied.

He was silent for a long time, looking at his desk and rubbing his forehead. I had obviously struck a sensitive nerve; after all, I was meddling in areas concerned with his own career. I expected the worst: I thought he was going to tell me to mind my own business or to find another job.

Finally, he looked at me and said firmly, "This is a dangerous undertaking, Nick. For you to enter those houses without any police protection is an act of insanity. How do we know what you are going to find inside and who might strike you? I will not allow you to go ahead with your quixotic plan."

I was taken aback by the firmness of his tone, but I recovered my composure rapidly. "I understand," I said, with equal firmness, "your position and responsibilities as the head of the Department of Public Security. I also understand your concern for my safety, and I am grateful. But this is a risk that I have to take and for which I have to assume full responsibility. I don't believe I'll get any worthwhile information if I go escorted by a policeman."

He tried to convince me to change my mind, but I stood my ground and reminded him that I had gone through a lot of dangerous situations before. Finally, he told me, "Go ahead and do what you have to do; but if something happens to you, don't blame me."

A week later, I selected what was considered one of the best houses in the Zone for my first inspection tour. This house had the reputation of attracting the prettiest girls and the best customers. Of special interest to me was a beautiful seventeen-year-old girl named Josefina who was working in that house and whom I had seen at the clinic that week. She had gonorrhea and a vulvar ulcer; the latter could have been either the first stage of syphilis or an acute chancroid. Since I needed time to make the correct diagnosis, I had told the girl, and also sent a note to her madam, that under no circumstances should she work for at least two weeks.

I entered the house shortly after 8:00 P.M. and found myself face to face with the madam, who was sitting on a chair by the main door. She recognized me and smiled. She was certain that the object of my visit was sexual pleasure and not medical inspection. She welcomed me warmly. "You are honoring me and my house, doctor. Would you like to have a glass of champagne with me before you look over my precious collection?"

I thanked her and said, "Do you mind if I inspect your rooms and hygiene facilities?"

A look of apprehension clouded her face. "But, doctor, the rooms are all occupied and I have no way of showing you anything," she said pleadingly.

In a large room across the way, some of the girls were sitting around a table, and others were standing by the window trying to entice the men passing in the street.

"This can't be true. Most of the girls are still here," I said. "I want to see the rooms and the toilet facilities."

She finally guided me down a corridor and opened one of the doors to show me a room. I was stunned. It was a cubicle barely large enough to contain a rusty cot, on which lay a thin, filthy mattress. Next to the cot, a bowl of dirty water was sitting on a rusty metal stand. A few filthy rags that served as towels hung on the wall.

For a few minutes I could not articulate my feelings. At last I said, "I am sure this is where the maid lives. Could you show me where the girls do their regular work and where they and their customers clean themselves afterward?"

"I'm sorry," she answered, "but all our rooms are like this."

"Could you show me the toilet facilities?" I asked.

She walked in front of me to the rear of the building, where there were two small shacks. The one used by the girls contained a toilet without a cover. The water tank was attached high on the wall behind the toilet and a long rope was tied to the tank handle. There was no sink or faucet. In the next shack, which served for the men, there was only a small cement area against the wall, leading to a basin and a drain in the ground. There was only one shower and it could be used only by some of the girls and the madam.

Back in the house, I looked for Josefina among the girls in the waiting room, but did not see her. I presumed that she had followed my advice with the madam's consent and had gone home. But on my way out, I passed by the waiting room again, and there was Josefina in her negligee, enticing a man through the window.

I turned to the madam and said, "I thought I had sent you an official warning to isolate that girl and not allow her to work." Then I called Josefina and said, "Why are you working?"

She blushed, and the madam added quickly: "Doctor, we have to pay the rent. These girls have to eat and buy clothes. We can't stop working; we have a lot of bills to pay."

I almost screamed at her: "Do you realize what you are doing to this girl and to the men who have sex with her? You are responsible for the spread of venereal diseases in this community!"

My heated argument with the madam at the main entrance attracted the attention of the girls in the waiting room and of some men in the cubicles. Various doors flung open and heads popped out. The madam had become almost hysterical and was shouting threats and insults at me.

I walked out, grabbed the first police officer I met in the street, identified myself, and asked him to follow me to the house. At this point the madam lost all sense of self-respect and composure. She banged her fists against the wall, she screamed obscenities, and she threatened to go to the governor. I paid no attention to her and ordered the police officer to take Josefina to the clinic immediately.

Behind my desk in the clinic, I faced that poor girl. She was crying and shivering, not from cold, but from terror. I patted her head, gave her some coffee, and tried to calm her as best I could. With the exception of one nurse who was on duty that night, we were alone.

Having relaxed a little, Josefina asked what I planned to do with her. I looked at that young, frail, and frightened girl, with her pretty face, her black hair, and her blue eyes. Suddenly, I felt overwhelmed by a sense of pity for her and disgust for the society that had dragged her into such an abject pit. "Josefina," I said, "you have to trust me; my only intention is to cure you of the diseases that are wrecking your body and to prevent you from getting them again. You are so young and beautiful, and you have many years to live. If I can help make those years happier and your life more bearable, I will."

She was crying again. The tears made her eyes more sparkling and more gorgeous against a face that reflected nothing but agony and torment.

After she had stopped crying, I said, "Josefina, maybe you'd like to tell me something about your life."

She seemed uneasy. "Will you promise not to tell the madam?" she asked hesitantly. When I agreed, she started talking.

She came from a large poor family who lived in the slums of São Paulo. She had two younger sisters and three brothers. Her father was a factory worker, and his salary was not enough to buy food for the family. Her mother was a house cleaner when she could find a job. They lived in a two-room shack which was part of a large tenement belonging to a rich landlord by the name of Senhor Mario. To help support the family, her father had forced her to leave school to go to work in the factory where he was employed. When she reported to the main office at the factory, she was surprised to see Senhor Mario there. He told her that he was the owner of the factory, and he would give her a good job if she promised to be "a good girl."

Next day she started to work in the main office as a cleaner. Senhor Mario told her that the job was temporary and that he would give her another one as soon as it became available. Several weeks later, he told her that he now needed her to clean his apartment. In his car he took her to his extravagant apartment downtown. He offered to pick her up from home and bring her to his apartment four times a week, but she had to take the bus back when she finished her work. Her salary was tripled. Three weeks later, Senhor Mario told her that he was pleased with her work and presented her with a beautiful gold necklace. He also bought her new clothes and high-heeled shoes so that she would look presentable when she was seen with him in the car or in the apartment, although nobody ever came to the apartment when she was there.

One day, Senhor Mario returned to the apartment for lunch and invited her to join him. She felt flattered. They drank champagne before lunch and wine with the meal and she got drunk. He suddenly started kissing her, fondling her breasts, and before long the two of them were in bed. Lunch at the apartment and sexual orgies became routine for Senhor Mario and Josefina during the next few weeks, until one day Josefina told him she might be pregnant. He took her to a doctor, who confirmed it.

On the following day, Senhor Mario called her father to the factory office and told him that his daughter had been sleeping with the janitor of his apartment building and that he had caught her with him in his own bed. "I am sorry but she can no longer work for me."

That night, Josefina got the worst beating she ever had from her father. She was bruised all over her body and both of her eyes were swollen and black; blood was streaming from her nose. The more she tried to explain to her father, the more infuriated he became, because she was defaming an "honorable man." After he tired of beating her, he opened the front door and kicked her out. "There is no room in my house for a whore!" he screamed.

Josefina was in a daze. She walked aimlessly through

the night and ended up at the bus station. She wanted to go away but did not know where. She searched her pockets but found no money for bus fare.

Suddenly, a middle-aged, heavily made-up woman appeared from nowhere. She spoke to Josefina in a sweet, soft voice: my poor child—you've been beaten badly—look at your body and face—how they are bruised—your nose is bleeding—what brute beat you so badly?—let me take you to my home, my child, and heal your wounds. And before Josefina could say a word, the nice lady waved to a chauffeur-driven car by the curb; she pushed Josefina into the back seat and sat next to her, soothing her with kind words and drying her tears with a perfumed handkerchief.

They drove to a beautiful house in one of the wealthiest neighborhoods. The lady helped Josefina shed her torn and dirty clothes, cleaned her body with warm perfumed water, and covered her bruises with ointment. She gave her something to eat and put her in a clean and comfortable bed.

Two days later, while having breakfast, the lady said: "My child, you feel much better now, don't you? But you are pregnant, aren't you? If you wish, you may call me mother."

Startled, Josefina said: "Yes, I am pregnant, but how did you find out?"

"I felt your stomach while I was cleaning you and putting ointment on your skin," the lady said. "We have to do something about that before it gets bigger. I wouldn't let you fall in disgrace; your father would kill you."

That same week, the lady took Josefina to the home of a midwife in a rundown section of the town. The midwife had a special room prepared with a bed, instrument table, sponges, and cotton. After placing her flat on the bed, the midwife shoved an instrument into Josefina's vagina. Without anesthesia or pain reliever, the midwife inserted a small round object made of wood into the mouth of her womb. This procedure caused incredible pain. The midwife and the lady told Josefina that it would take six to eight hours. The lady added, "You'll have a lot of pain and lose some blood, my child, but you have to be brave." She gave her a towel to put in her mouth when the pains became severe and she wanted to cry out.

Josefina spent the next eight hours in agony; every time she wanted to scream, the two women covered her mouth with the towel. Finally, she gave a loud scream and a hard push and expelled something from her vagina. She then passed out.

She did not know how long she was unconscious. When she awoke, she was in bed in the home of the lady. She was still losing blood and felt feverish. A doctor who examined her said that parts of the afterbirth were still inside the uterus and moved her to a hospital. He scraped her uterus and gave her a blood transfusion. Two days later the lady brought her back to her home.

Josefina began regaining her strength. Two weeks after the operation, the lady presented her with several bills: one from the midwife for $200; one from the doctor for $400; one from the hospital for $500; and one for an itemized list of clothes for $800. "My child," said the lady, "I have spent a lot of money to save you from disgrace and to get you back to normal. Look at all these bills! I have to pay them. I know you don't have any money, but you are young and beautiful. With your gorgeous figure, you can make millions and you can have diamonds, gold, and glamorous clothes. Maybe you can become a movie star."

Josefina felt overwhelmed. Ten days later, the lady

took her to the house in the Zone and introduced her to the other girls, who taught her the details of the business. It was not long before Josefina began using her body for business. The lady who had taken care of her all those days turned out to be the madam of the house. She asked her to turn over every dollar she made to her for safe-keeping.

Josefina had been in the Zone for only two months when she noticed the ulcer on her vulva and the purulent discharge from her vagina. And that was when the madam told her to see me at the clinic.

It was past 2:00 A.M. when Josefina finished telling me her story. I took her to one of the rooms in the clinic and told her to sleep there.

The tragic story of that young girl and the sight of that house disturbed me profoundly. The problems that I had faced in my youth seemed pale in comparison. How much cruelty could there be in this world?

Prostitution is a corrupt and filthy business; yet, I asked myself, is it any more corrupt and filthy than what I had witnessed in steel and coal mines, cotton mills and textile factories? Is manufacturing and selling arms that kill people a more legitimate business than selling sex to satisfy man's physiological function? Certainly, prostitution is the main source of venereal diseases, but are these diseases any worse than lung ailments contracted in mines and factories? At least now we can cure gonorrhea and syphilis. But what can we do for lung cancer?

These painful questions haunted me that night, and they were to continue to haunt me throughout the two years of my stay among the prostitutes.

The following morning I decided to cure Josefina as fast as possible and use her as an example to encourage other sick girls to come to the clinic and seek treatment; I would try to help Josefina out of her predicament and improve the hygienic conditions of the Zone through legal channels.

By 1944 it was established that massive doses of penicillin could cure syphilis and gonorrhea. But the supply of penicillin in Brazil was small and its use was limited to extreme emergencies in the armed services. I called Alfredo at his house that morning and reported on my inspection of the house. "I need you to help me get penicillin from the government's stock," I said.

"I will call you back in about an hour," Alfredo answered.

Meanwhile, I issued an order that Josefina was not to leave the clinic under any circumstances; I placed her under Carina's care. I did not have the correct diagnosis of Josefina's vulvar lesion, but I assumed it to be primary syphilis.

Alfredo obtained the release of 200 million units of penicillin, and an hour later I injected Josefina with the first million units. The same amount was administered over five subsequent days.

One week later, Josefina was cured of gonorrhea and her vulvar lesion had shrunk to a small scar. By that time, I already had the exact diagnosis of primary syphilis.

In view of the successful treatment of Josefina with penicillin, I decided to have another meeting with the madams to tell them about the new treatment. At the same time, I thought, I would appeal to them to improve the hygienic conditions of their houses.

On the appointed day, all the madams assembled. I showed them the penicillin vial and said, "This stuff cures gonorrhea and syphilis in five days, *provided* early diagnosis of the illnesses is made. If one of you doubts my words, I am willing to let you question and even examine Josefina; she is totally cured now."

They were pleased with the news and promised to

send their girls for weekly checkups at the clinic.

I proceeded to tell them that in order to eliminate the diseases altogether, hygienic improvements had to be made. "That includes proper toilet facilities, disinfecting, and the elementary procedures that every girl can use to check whether a man has a venereal disease before she has relations with him."

We kept Josefina working at the clinic for about two months, but suddenly, she disappeared. I found out later that she was induced to return to prostitution.

My struggle to reform the system and diminish the incidence of venereal diseases continued for two years, with varying degrees of success—not enough to satisfy me. And just as I grew discouraged about my ability to reform the system of prostitution, something happened that changed my life completely.

13 · Alfredo's Illness

By the end of 1944, my cousin Alfredo had reached a very high position in the state government. In importance and prestige he actually overshadowed the aging and inept governor. Although Alfredo was barely thirty-five, he was considered a possible candidate for governor of the state of São Paulo, or minister of justice in the Vargas government. He had written two books on law and justice, which were much admired by many Latin American jurists.

Just after the New Year's celebrations, Alfredo began complaining of abdominal discomfort followed by bouts of diarrhea. He confided his health problems to one of his friends, who happened to be a doctor. The doctor assured him that it was nothing serious and, without examining him, diagnosed possible anal fissures or hemorrhoids and prescribed some medication to be applied to the rectum.

As often happens with important people, Alfredo's illness was kept secret from everyone, including his mother and relatives; in addition to the doctor, the only persons who knew about it were his bodyguard and his secretary. Meanwhile, the medicine prescribed by the doctor apparently had no effect, and the rectal bleeding got worse.

One evening Alfredo was having dinner at the home

of his mother, who had married my Uncle George not too long after his wife's death. I was also invited. During the dinner Alfredo had to go to the toilet. A few minutes later he called me. His face was pale, his forehead drenched with cold sweat. In the toilet bowl, in the middle of a pool of blood, there was stool mixed with both fresh and clotted blood. Obviously Alfredo was seriously ill. I asked him how long this had been going on. He said about three months.

The next day Alfredo was admitted to the hospital and underwent a series of radiographic and rectosigmoidoscopic examinations. All showed cancer of the descending colon. The news spread quickly through all of Brazil. Because of his prominence, there was considerable indecision about who should perform the necessary surgery, and whether it should be done in Brazil or the United States. Finally, Professor Vasconcellos, chairman of surgery at the University of São Paulo, was selected.

Vasconcellos had been my professor of surgical technique, and I knew him well. He was something of a showman, concerned more with the technical perfection of the surgical act itself than with the end result. Obsessed with the speed with which he could perform major surgical procedures, he was the prototype of what we call the "lightning-fast slash-and-stitch" surgeon. And so I was not happy with the choice, but could do nothing about it.

On the day of the operation the hospital was jammed with important people. The area surrounding the operating room was like an armed camp, with police and secret service everywhere. The doctor who had been treating my cousin and I were allowed to stand inside the operating room. Vasconcellos made the abdominal incision, which, to me, appeared too small for adequate exploration for abdominal metastasis, or spread, of the cancer. He reached the tumor, excised it, diverted the bowel through the skin, and was ready to close the skin over the operative wound in less than forty-five minutes. I did not see him reach in with his hand to explore the abdominal cavity for additional tumors. Needless to say, I was most unhappy about the procedure, but could not express my feelings to anyone; it was important now to lift Alfredo's spirits.

The postoperative course was uneventful, and Alfredo left the hospital after three weeks; he began recuperating at the home of Uncle George, who was now his stepfather. But hardly had he recovered enough to go out— three months after surgery—when the first enlarged lymph node was felt in his inguinal area. He showed me the lump and asked what it was. I tried to maintain my composure, even though I was certain of the diagnosis. I told him it was probably tissue reaction to the operation.

Not long afterward, however, other lumps started appearing in different areas of his abdomen. By that time everyone, including Alfredo, knew that the cancer was spreading fast and further treatment was needed. A group of doctors, professors from universities in Rio and São Paulo, were assembled for consultation. It was decided that he should go to the United States, specifically to the Chicago Radium Institute, for radiation therapy. At that time Brazil had no such facilities. Although I was convinced it was a mistake to send him anywhere, again there was nothing I could do about it.

The Brazilian government altered a DC-3 airplane into a sort of ambulance and placed it at Alfredo's service. After considerable deliberation, I was selected to accompany him.

My separation from Carina was painful for both of us. We spent our last night in each other's arms. Carina had

an intuitive feeling that I would never come back. I then
went to say good-bye to my little boy, Robin. I told his
mother that if she needed anything she should turn to
my brothers.

My mother was not too happy about my departure.
She kissed me good-bye and said, "I hope you'll return
in a few months. I've told your brothers to make a position for you in the store. If you don't like it, they'll help
you open an office for yourself. You'll need money after
you come back!"

Part Three

THE
UNITED
STATES

14 · *Alfredo's Last Days*

THE DC-3 took off from the São Paulo airport on June 20, 1945. The cabin had a bed for Alfredo, three seats joined together for me, and similar arrangements for the two male stewards who accompanied us. Although the plane was pressurized, it had no heat or air conditioning. Consequently, we reached our first stop, Belém, in the north of Brazil, with the temperature about 110 degrees and a humidity of ninety to one hundred percent. Alfredo was suffering from the heat, as well as from the inexorable cancer.

We spent the night in Belém, because in those days commercial flying at night hardly existed. The hotel was mediocre, but it was cooler than the airplane cabin. The flight continued in the morning, and by noon, as we neared the equator, the heat and humidity were unbearable. Somehow we managed to survive until landing at Panama, where we slept overnight. We left the following morning and, after another stop, finally reached Miami late in the afternoon, where again we stayed overnight. We arrived in Chicago the next morning. An ambulance was waiting for us at the airport, and both Alfredo and I went directly to Michael Reese Hospital, where he was admitted as a patient. I got a room at the Drake Hotel.

A series of laboratory tests, radiographic examinations, and biopsies of the enlarged nodes confirmed the diagnosis of widespread cancer. The doctors told me that any treatment would be palliative, and that the chance for cure was zero. They agreed with me that it was a mistake to have brought him to the United States. Most people are afraid to die, but Alfredo had more fear than anyone I knew; he had expressed these fears, particularly of cancer, to me and to others. So my problem, at least for the first few weeks, was to keep his hopes and morale high by hiding the truth. The American doctors were most helpful in this regard. Although they believed as a rule that the patient should be told the truth, in his case they made an exception.

The radiation treatment was to be carried out at the Chicago Radium Institute, only one block from the Drake Hotel. To simplify matters, we moved Alfredo to the Drake, where we took a large apartment. And so I began the painful task of coping with the physical and emotional problems of my dying relative and friend.

The first three weeks were relatively simple because the pain had not as yet become too severe. Codeine and occasional injections of mild sedatives were sufficient to keep him comfortable. Each day I would give him his breakfast and then accompany him in a taxi to the Institute. Except to go to the Institute, we never left the apartment.

After the third week, the pains increased, and Alfredo had lumps in many areas of his body, including the liver. He became jaundiced and slowly lost his appetite. He also lost control of his bowel movements, and the bed was constantly soiled with diarrhetic stools mixed with blood. I stayed close to him all the time and increased the number of injections of strong sedatives. Walking to and from the taxi, or taking the few steps to and from the main building of the Institute, became extremely difficult for him, so finally I had to get a wheelchair.

Both the pains of cancer and the debilitating effects of the radiation treatment began taking their toll on Alfredo's strength. Neither the sedatives nor the sleeping pills produced any prolonged effects. He began asking me for more injections and stronger pills practically every hour of the day and night. I did not hesitate to give him anything he wanted, even though the medical ethics of that time opposed letting the patient become dependent on heavy sedation. Since Alfredo was dying, I thought it my obligation to keep him as comfortable as possible and forget about dependency and ethics. Finally I hired a male nurse to help me care for him. This was a wise move, because the nurse relieved me of some of the hard night work and I could get some sleep.

We had been at the Drake Hotel for over two months. Alfredo's condition was getting worse every day and I myself was literally exhausted. Since the radiation treatment did no good and the end grew closer, we decided Alfredo should return to Michael Reese Hospital. This second admission, around the middle of August, was a blessing for me: I went back to the hotel and slept for twenty-four hours.

By the end of August, Alfredo was reduced to skin and bones. His pain was unbearable and couldn't be relieved by any sedatives. I had abandoned all religious beliefs and become an atheist a long time before this, but when I heard him screaming from pain and begging me to help him, I went into the hall and prayed to God to put a speedy end to Alfredo's misery.

Whether God heard me or not, an act of mercy occurred two days later. I was sitting next to his bed, holding his hand. He had been given a sedative injection a few minutes before. Suddenly he became extremely lucid and serene. He looked at me, and I saw tears rolling down his cheeks. He pressed my hand warmly and said:

"Thanks for all you did, Nick. No one could have done as much." A few minutes later, he lapsed into a coma and became unconscious and insensitive to pain. Two days later this bright young man, who had reached so high a position so quickly and on whom so much hope had been placed, died.

I wired his mother and informed the Brazilian government through its consul in Chicago. Twenty-four hours later I received through the consul official orders from the office of President Vargas to make all necessary preparations for Alfredo's body to be shipped back to Brazil.

I did not attend the funeral services for Alfredo. My family told me that he received honors and memorial ceremonies accorded to only a very few in Brazil up to that time. A street in São Paulo now bears his name.

15 · Search for a Job

DURING the agonizing days and nights that I spent caring for Alfredo in Chicago, I made up my mind to stay in the United States for one year. I wanted to observe how medicine was practiced there and what was new in obstetrics, particularly in regard to toxemia of pregnancy.

Prior to World War II, United States medicine was little known in Brazil and other Latin American countries. The teaching and practice of medicine was modeled in large part on the French and German schools, because most of our professors had gone to Germany for additional training.

But the picture changed rapidly during the war, and particularly after the defeat of Germany. American textbooks had replaced German ones in all branches of medicine, and American medical journals were now being read by professors and students alike. Young doctors eager to pursue academic and research careers sought positions in American universities—a trend that was considerably encouraged by exchange fellowships and programs established by the American government and by private American philanthropic organizations. Prominent among the organizations offering fellowships in American universities were the Institute of International Education, the Rockefeller Foundation, the Guggenheim Foundation, and the Fulbright program. I knew several doctors who had gone to American universities for additional training. Although the majority had nothing but praise for it, particularly for medical research, others—mostly surgeons—commented unfavorably on the skills of American surgeons.

After Alfredo's death I moved to the YMCA and started writing letters to various foundations. The Institute of International Education was at the top of my list, because I had studied English at night at its São Paulo branch. I wrote to its director for an introduction to the main office in New York, and he sent me an excellent recommendation. I also obtained letters from some of my professors at the university and copies of my medical-school records.

Armed with all this documentation, I left for New York to have an interview at the Institute of International Education and to make an official application for a fellowship. My interview went well, and I was told that the decision would be reached within a week. Meanwhile, I visited various medical centers, including Columbia University, Mount Sinai, and Bellevue Hospital, but because my visits were informal, I was unable to gain access to any of the teaching staff. Ten days later I was officially notified that I had been awarded a fellowship by the Institute of International Education.

The Institute had a list of hospitals, mostly private, that had requested foreign fellows for clinical work. A few research positions in different universities were also listed, but they were mostly in basic sciences, internal medicine, and pediatrics; none in obstetrics. This was strange and ominous, I thought. There was a specialty that offered great possibilities for research, yet even the Institute did not include it in its program.

Nevertheless, I convinced the Institute that I could

find a position if they allowed me to look around. After a lot of negotiating, I was permitted to visit the various departments at East Coast universities from Washington to Boston; I was also allowed to include the University of Michigan.

Since I was in New York, I decided to look over its universities first. I went to Columbia and talked to the department chairman and his associates. I observed their management of obstetrical complications, including toxemia, but nothing I saw differed from what we did in Brazil. I inquired about research in obstetrics, but was only presented with statistical compilations, reports of unusual cases, and morphological studies of specimens, particularly of genital cancer. I asked Professor B. Watson, who was chairman at that time, whether it would be possible for me to try some physiological investigations; he referred me to other departments—mainly internal medicine, physiology, and pharmacology. I encountered the same situation and received similar answers at Cornell and at New York University, as well as at private hospitals.

I left New York for Washington, D.C., where I visited two universities and the city's general hospital. In the latter I observed numerous cases of toxemia of pregnancy, handled mostly by the house staff. Again I saw the same procedures, with emphasis on heavy sedation and other palliative treatment. Research beyond statistical compilations was out of the question.

Johns Hopkins University, in Baltimore, was probably the most famous hospital of all, and the best known in Brazil. There the Obstetrics Department, which was separate from the Gynecology Department, was headed by Dr. Nicholson Eastman, a highly respected man. Dr. Emil Novak, at that time the most respected gynecologist in the world, was also on the staff of Johns Hopkins.

I had special letters of introduction to both men. I was certain that at Johns Hopkins I would finally find what I was looking for.

Dr. Eastman received me cordially in his office and asked me to make rounds with him and the house staff. As we walked toward the obstetrical ward, he put his arm around me—a gesture that was Eastman's trademark, and that I was to experience many times during the twenty or more years of our friendship. He visited each patient and talked and joked with his house staff and students in a warm, informal manner. How different, I thought, from Brazilian universities! Finally we reached a patient with severe toxemia, high blood pressure, albumin in the urine, and extreme swelling of her whole body. He promptly asked me how we managed such cases in Brazil. I told him we prescribed heavy sedation with morphine or chloral hydrate, some magnesium sulfate, and bed rest, and we delivered the patient as soon as we could. "That's just how we handle it," he said. "You aren't too far behind. Why are you here then?"

Dr. Eastman took me out to lunch. I asked him if I could do some work in his department, both clinical and research. I wished to investigate, I told him, why young women develop such a fulminating hypertensive disorder. He warned me that this disease had puzzled many people for a long time and that no one had been able to make any headway. Moreover, he pointed out—politely —that there was no room for research on these patients in his department.

A few days later I returned to Johns Hopkins Hospital and asked for Professor Novak. "Professor who?" asked the information clerk.

"Professor Novak," I answered, "the famous gynecologist."

"Dr. Novak works at Bon Secour Hospital; he rarely

comes here," she said. "If you want to talk to him, you'll have to go there."

I was certain she was wrong. Novak was known all over the world as one of Johns Hopkins's most illustrious men. How could he come there "rarely"?

I decided to ask one of Dr. Eastman's assistants with whom I had become friendly. He confirmed what the clerk had said and told me confidentially that the famous Dr. Novak was not even allowed to bring patients to Johns Hopkins. He was allowed only to examine some pathological slides but not to take them out, and that he did all his work in his office and in a couple of private hospitals. I felt depressed and disillusioned. To this day I do not understand why Dr. Novak was allowed to state in his book and publications that he was a member of the faculty, but not allowed to bring patients to the hospital.

I made an appointment to see Dr. Novak at Bon Secour Hospital. He was kind and charming. He invited me to watch him perform a vaginal hysterectomy. Although observing gynecological surgery was not much to my liking, I agreed as a matter of courtesy. He started the operation with the help of two young black residents; in a short time there was so much blood that I was unable to see a thing. I did not think him a very skilled surgeon.

I next made a brief visit to Yale University. The department chairman was out of town, and there was nothing going on in obstetrics except improvement in radiographic measurements of the pelvis. Since Yale's Department of Internal Medicine was famous for its work on water and electrolyte metabolisms and the mechanisms of edema, I visited that department before leaving for Boston.

Boston was another center in which I had invested great hope. The Lying-In Hospital, a part of Harvard Medical School, was as famous as Johns Hopkins, and in

some areas more so. I had a special letter of introduction
to Dr. Fritz Irving, the chairman of obstetrics and head
of the hospital. He received me with kindness, then took
me around and showed me the hospital, including the
pediatrics division. I asked for his thoughts on toxemia
and current research. "We're just as lost as everybody
else," he answered. "As for research, Dr. Arthur Hertig
is studying the placenta of toxemia patients. For treatment we use the same old stuff—heavy sedation, magnesium sulfate, and bed rest." He paused, then continued:
"We're just beginning now to administer a preparation
called Veratrone, made by Parke, Davis and Company.
We inject it into the muscle in small doses. It certainly
brings the blood pressure down, but that's all we know."

Here was the first new variation in the treatment of
toxemia that I had heard of up to that time, and I was
excited. "Do you know if anybody else uses this preparation?" I asked.

"Oh yes," he said. "A group of obstetricians in Cincinnati has for years. They claim the lowest maternal mortality from convulsive toxemia [eclampsia] in the world.
Many people doubt their statistics, but we thought we'd
try their method, for lack of anything better." He told
me that if I stayed until they had a case of toxemia, I
could watch them using Veratrone.

I asked if by any chance there was an opening for me
in his department. He said that he would be retiring in
a few months and would leave the hiring and firing to
the new chairman.

As it turned out, no patient with toxemia was admitted for the ten days I was in Boston. But my time wasn't
wasted. I met Dr. Hertig and watched him at work on
the placenta. The sight of him bent over the microscope
for hours on end frightened me, and I realized once and
for all I could never do that type of work. Hertig and I

developed a friendship, however, that was to last a lifetime. I also visited the Pharmacology Department and met Professor Otto Krayer and his associates, who were working on the veratrum alkaloids. I had read everything they had published, as well as the report of Drs. Richard Bryant and John Fleming, in Cincinnati, on the use of veratrum viride in eclampsia. I was greatly impressed by Bryant and Fleming's reported maternal mortality of less than two percent in true cases of eclampsia. Even given an error by a factor of two, it would still be an improvement over the average world mortality rate of ten percent.

It was Christmastime and I was lonely in Boston. One of my sisters lived in a small town near Montreal, so I decided to visit her. I spent two wonderful weeks with her and her family. I also visited the laboratories, at McGill University, of Professor Hans Selye, whose work on experimental nephrosclerosis (a disease that transforms most of the kidney tissue into scar tissue and leads to the development of high blood pressure) in rats had impressed me a great deal, and called on the departments of obstetrics and gynecology of both McGill and the French University of Montreal. Then I left for the University of Michigan, in Ann Arbor, the last place on my itinerary. Since my other sister lived in Detroit, I decided to commute from Detroit to the university.

On the train from Montreal to Detroit, I reconstructed my discussions with the various scientists I had recently met. To me the development of sudden high blood pressure in young pregnant women emerged as a key to the general problem of hypertension in man. I became obsessed with the idea that if the cause of hypertension in toxemia could be found, the door would be opened to an understanding of the entire spectrum of hypertensive diseases. I began to have grave doubts about the classical teaching in obstetrics. I had been taught by the professors in Brazil, and told by those with whom I discussed toxemia in the United States, that one should not worry about the hypertension or treat it. The rise in blood pressure, they said, was "compensatory" and kept the blood flowing to organs and tissues. This was an old concept, which in the light of new research was being discarded by investigators in the field of hypertension. Yet the majority of obstetricians held firmly to it; many of them considered it an act of insanity to try to lower the blood pressure. Some of them still hold this belief today, despite overwhelming evidence to the contrary.

After resting for a couple of days at my sister's house in Detroit, I went to Ann Arbor to visit the Obstetrics and Gynecology Department of the University of Michigan. Dr. Norman Miller, the chairman, received me warmly. He took me on the usual tour of his facilities and showed me the plans for a new building, soon to be constructed, that would be strictly for the department's use.

After a brief conversation, I realized that Dr. Miller's main interest was not in obstetric research but in the follow-up of patients with cancer of the cervix. He showed me his perfected method for keeping track of these patients over the past eighteen years. He brought patients back for checkups even from distant parts of the country by enlisting the help of the police, the church, various health departments, and whatever other agency he could. I marveled at his perseverance and concern. He offered me a position in his cancer program, but I declined with much regret. My interest was in obstetric research.

In Ann Arbor I visited the hypertension clinic in the Department of Medicine and learned about their concept of blood-pressure rise and its management. I also traveled to Cleveland to visit the great hypertension center, headed at that time by Irving Page. By talking to him and to his collaborator Arthur Corcoran and their co-workers, I learned a great deal about the pathogenesis and treatment of hypertension. Just as I was leaving the Cleveland clinic, Page turned to me and said, "This is the first time we've had an obstetrician inquiring about hypertension. If hypertension of pregnancy could be elucidated, the whole problem of hypertension would be solved." To this day I remember those words.

I returned to Detroit and wondered what to do next. The answer came quickly when I analyzed what had been accomplished so far. On the one hand, I was exhilarated by the information I had acquired in Boston and from conversations with investigators in the field of hypertension. I felt that obstetricians' thinking was far wide of the mark, and that their approach to the management of toxemia of pregnancy had no sound basis. On the other hand, I had no way to test or prove any hypothesis of my own, because I had failed to find a place to work. I knew it would be impossible for me to test anything in Brazil. The place to do it was here in the United States. But where?

I had reached the end of the line with the Institute of International Education. They had allowed me freedom of choice. It was time either to confess my failure and return to Brazil or to accept one of the positions the Institute had available.

16 · Research Work in Cincinnati

ONE morning toward the end of January 1946 I got up, went to a gas station near my sister's house, and asked for a map of the Midwest. I looked for Cincinnati; it was only 250 miles from Detroit. I called the Institute in New York and asked permission to visit the University of Cincinnati. I promised that this would be my last try and that I would make a final decision after that. The following day I took the train and arrived in Cincinnati that night. As usual, I stayed at the YMCA.

The next morning I went to Cincinnati General Hospital, where the Obstetrics Department of the university was located. I walked into huge wards that reminded me of the wards in the hospital in São Paulo. Each ward consisted of a long hall with fifty or sixty beds against the walls. Pregnant patients with complications and postpartum patients were in the same ward. Between the two sections were the nursery and the labor and delivery rooms. The lack of medical staff struck me right away. Two residents and three interns were making rounds accompanied by only three nurses. This was in contrast to other departments I had visited, where the chairman and his senior associates were present practically all the time.

I told Dr. Henry Woodward, the chairman, that I had heard in Boston about his group's treatment of toxemia.

"I'm glad other people are getting interested in our method," he said. "It's about time."

I asked if there was any chance I could investigate their method of treatment. He answered: "The university has no money to hire anyone. Except for the residents and interns, we're all here part-time. I'm retiring within a few months and the new chairman, whoever he turns out to be, will probably have different ideas." After more talk he added, "But there is a private hospital here, Bethesda. Most of our faculty, including myself, take our private patients there, and we manage toxemia in the same way. Why not work there? They need people and they pay well." Dr. Woodward's suggestion sounded attractive. I called the Institute of International Education in New York for their approval and they promptly gave it. And after an interview at Bethesda Hospital, I was hired as a fellow in obstetrics and gynecology.

My first three months at Bethesda Hospital were spent in the maternity pavilion. The first person I met there was the chief of obstetrics, Dr. Lloyd Zacharias. He was an honest and sincere person, with no pretensions. Although his theoretical knowledge of the field was limited, he was an excellent practical teacher at the bedside and in the delivery room. The two of us quickly became friends and remained so until his death in the mid-1960s.

Two weeks after I had started, the first case of severe pre-eclampsia was admitted, with a blood pressure of about 180/120 millimeters of mercury, a lot of swelling, and albumin in the urine. I was eager to see how she would be treated. Dr. Zacharias—Zac, as I came to call him—took an ugly bottle of Veratrone, whose contents were not even sterile, aspirated about one-fourth of a cubic centimeter into a syringe, and injected it intramuscularly into the patient. He also gave her some magnesium sulfate and a small dose of a sedative, Seconal. He asked me to keep taking the blood pressure every five minutes. Within fifteen minutes after the injection, the blood pressure had fallen to normal levels of about 120/80. The patient remained alert, unlike the women I had seen treated in other institutions, who became almost unconscious from the heavy sedation. Zac instructed me to repeat the dose of Veratrone whenever the blood pressure began to rise again.

The patient received three or four doses of the drug over the next twenty-four hours; she experienced nausea and occasional vomiting, some of the mysterious side effects of Veratrone. But after the first twenty-four hours the patient's swelling began to subside. She remained alert and in good spirits. Her kidneys began functioning well and putting out a lot of urine, and her blood pressure stabilized at normal levels. Since her baby was large and close to term, labor was induced and she had a normal delivery. I asked Zac, "Do you know how this stuff works?"

"No," he answered.

One month later a patient with convulsive eclampsia was admitted. She had suffered several convulsions at home and four or five more on arrival at the hospital. She was in a coma, with severe swelling; her kidneys were not putting out urine at all. The death rate for patients in this condition was high all over the world; I had seen many of them die in Brazil within twenty-four hours of admission. I was on duty that day and called Zac for help. The nurses and I had taken care of the ordinary measures, such as clearing her airways, giving her oxygen to breathe, and putting her in a quiet room. Zac calmly injected the patient with one-fourth cc of Veratrone in the muscle and gave her magnesium sulfate and some barbiturate—much the same treatment that the other patient, who was not as critically ill, had received. I recorded her blood pressure every two or three minutes. Before the Veratrone injection it was 210/110; thirty minutes after the injection it was 150/90. The patient had one more convulsion shortly after she received the injection, but Zac said not to worry. One hour after the first injection her blood pressure started climbing again. Zac told me to give her another injection. She vomited some, but without any serious consequences. The patient received more injections of magnesium sulfate and Veratrone over the next twenty-four hours. No more convulsions occurred. Slowly she began to regain consciousness, and her kidneys started putting out urine. Three days later she was eliminating her edema and was totally conscious; her blood pressure had stabilized at 140/90. She soon went into spontaneous labor and was delivered of a small but healthy baby.

I was now convinced that this treatment, which did not depend on heavy sedation but on lowering the blood pressure, was most effective, and I decided to make it my research area. However, my research could not be carried on at Bethesda Hospital, because all the patients there were private and under the supervision of their own physicians.

In the meantime I had become acquainted with Dr. Stanley Garber, who was Dr. Woodward's nephew and among the candidates considered for the department chairmanship. Garber told me that if he were selected, I was assured of a job at the university. I also met Bryant and Fleming, the two men who had published the first report on the management of eclampsia with veratrum viride. I thought Dr. Bryant was the sharpest of them all; he was inquisitive, took nothing for granted, and had an analytical mind. We discussed their report and I told them frankly that many people doubted their statistics. Bryant's answer was, "We know. Stick around and see for yourself."

While I was in obstetrics, Zac and I published a paper in the *American Journal of Obstetrics and Gynecology*, a statistical review of ten years' experience in the obstetrical service. We analyzed all the cases handled by obstetricians trained in the specialty and also those handled by general practitioners. The data showed a greater incidence of obstetrical complications, including severe cases of toxemia, infections, and pelvic relaxation, in the patients handled by general practitioners than in the cases handled by trained obstetricians. Before we sent the report to the journal, I presented the data to a general meeting of the medical staff of the hospital. Needless to say, the general practitioners were not pleased. But as a result of this report, a limitation was imposed on the types of obstetrical cases that the general practitioners could handle.

When I completed my three months' duties in obstetrics, I moved to gynecology and surgery. Gynecology at Bethesda Hospital was practiced almost entirely by surgeons. Consequently, there was very little clinical gynecology. The gynecological patients were admitted to the hospital after they had been seen and the diagnosis made in the doctor's private office. My job was largely limited to assisting the doctor in surgery.

This is where I had my first disappointment in the private practice of medicine in America; this is also where my troubles with some of the doctors began, troubles that were to cost me dearly in the future. I began seeing patients admitted for surgery who did not, in my opinion, need it at all. I purposely helped in the surgical procedures on these patients and saw many uteri, tubes, and ovaries, removed needlessly. It was particularly distressing to see a relatively young woman deprived of her uterus and ovaries and condemned to take hormones for much of her life. It was reminiscent of the experience I had had in São Paulo.

At first, I would speak to the doctor performing the operation. If that were my patient, I would say, I would not operate. In addition to the usual surgical risks, the anesthesia alone at that time carried a ten-percent mortality rate. After three months, I decided to take more drastic measures. I took some surgical specimens to the head of the clinical laboratories and discussed with him the absence of any real pathology justifying surgery. He and I decided to review the operative records of the hospital for a three-year period. We analyzed each patient's history, the indications for surgery, the findings during the operation, and the pathological examinations of the surgical specimens. The results of our survey were shocking: the vast majority of the uteri, ovaries, and tubes removed were without any abnormality.

We presented our findings at a monthly staff meeting, and created an uproar. Surgeons leaped to their feet and denounced us for making such statements. After all, we had not been involved in the clinical care of the patient and could not therefore know the whole story. They threatened that if the hospital administration allowed the report to be published, they would take their patients elsewhere. The following day the administration asked us to suppress the report, and we complied. A few months later, however, a paper was published in the *American Journal of Obstetrics and Gynecology* by none other than Professor Norman Miller, of the University of Michigan. He had reviewed the gynecological operations performed in ten major hospitals in the Midwest over a ten-year period and found that seventy percent of those operations were unnecessary.

Needless to say, my investigation did not endear me to the medical staff at Bethesda, particularly the gynecological surgeons.

17 · Formation of a Research Team

DR. STANLEY GARBER was selected the chairman of the Obstetrics Department at the University of Cincinnati. He promptly offered me a full-time job in teaching and research, but he told me that the university had no funds at all for faculty positions in the Obstetrical Department. Even Garber would be working without pay, like his predecessors.

"Any money to start the research program?" I asked.

"Not a nickel," was his answer.

I still had six more months on my fellowship, which paid $200 a month. Garber promised to pay me $100 a month from his own pocket and give me free room and board at the hospital. Research interested me more than money, so I accepted Garber's offer.

My first task at the hospital was to survey the Obstetrics Department in terms of research space and facilities, the staff coverage of the inpatient and outpatient departments, the teaching assignments, and the co-operation of the clinical faculty. The results were discouraging. First, Garber, the chairman, had one of the biggest and richest private practices in the city, which consumed practically all his time. For all intents and purposes, I was to cover most of his activities in the hospital. Second, there was no space to set up a research laboratory, even if the funds had been available. Third, there were from three hundred to four hundred deliveries a month, with a high percentage of complicated obstetrical cases, covered by only three or four residents and the same number of interns. The outpatient clinic was also handled by the residents, interns, and students; there was a list of faculty members on call for each clinic, but, with a few exceptions, they showed up only occasionally.

After this survey I had a long talk with Garber, and he and I spoke to the dean of the school, who promised to get us more residents and interns and some space for research. I was authorized to circulate a letter to the clinical attending staff asking for their co-operation in making rounds with the students and residents in the ward; I also requested their assistance and their observance of the assignments in the outpatient clinics. This letter produced some temporary results, and the clinical faculty began showing more interest in the department. In the area of teaching, I made a list of topics and assigned several students to the clinical faculty, including the chairman. I also asked the senior resident, Dr. Robert Kistner, who was to become professor of Obstetrics and Gynecology at Harvard Medical School and a world authority in the field, to take part in the teaching program, which would give him practice in teaching and in public speaking and force him to study the subject in depth. Within three months the teaching and patient-care program was on its way and improving steadily.

I could then turn my full attention to research. Since I was the only full-time person in the department, I had complete freedom to devise the research program as I saw fit. Because we had no space, equipment, or funds, I decided to seek collaboration with other departments. For the study of toxemia, I talked with Dr. Eugene Ferris, who was professor of internal medicine and chief of the division on hypertension. He was well-known and respected in his field. I convinced him that investigating the hypertension of young women with toxemia would be the key to the whole problem of hypertension, and Ferris put the resources of his division, which were considerable, at my disposal. I also got in touch with Dr. George Acheson, the new chairman of the Pharmacology Department, and he promised his full co-operation. He had worked with Dr. Krayer, at Harvard, on veratrum alkaloids. In the course of that investigation, Acheson and his colleague Gordon Moe had accidentally come upon a substance called tetraethyl ammonium chloride (TEAC). They observed that this substance, when injected intravenously, blocked all the nerve impulses going to the blood vessels; it was like performing chemical sympathectomy. Parke, Davis & Company began making this compound because they thought it would prove to be the key to treating hypertension. TEAC's action was too fleeting to be of practical use for patients, but it did have other uses and in time led to the development of other drugs for hypertension.

I was also able to engage the collaboration of Dr. Pearl Zeek, of the Department of Pathology, whose area of study was the changes in blood vessels produced by high blood pressure. She was enthusiastic at the prospect of studying the blood vessels of young women who had just developed fulminating hypertension. Our joint paper on the changes in the blood vessels of the uterus produced by toxemia was to become a classic in this field.

Ferris suggested a meeting of all the investigators to be involved in the research of hypertensive diseases of pregnancy. He asked me to organize the meeting, outline to the group my views on previous studies, and propose the problems to be investigated.

I analyzed the subject as follows: The concept held by obstetricians that the hypertension of toxemia is "com-

pensatory" and should not be treated is wrong. Therefore the hypertension of toxemia, its mechanisms, and
the impact of its management should be investigated.
But before investigating the mechanisms of the rise in
blood pressure in toxemia, how the blood pressure is
controlled in normal pregnancy must be investigated.
Obstetricians believe the renal functions in toxemia are
not greatly different from those of normal individuals.
This belief could be erroneous for two reasons: first, the
signs and symptoms of toxemia, including the dimin-
ished formation of urine and the swelling of the body,
point toward disturbed kidney functions; second, those
who studied renal functions in toxemia compared their
values to normal nonpregnant individuals. As in the case
of blood pressure, such a comparison is erroneous because the normal nonpregnant individual is different
from the normal pregnant one. Our control group
should be normal pregnant subjects with the same period of gestation.

We should study the blood flow to organs and tissues,
particularly to the uterus and placenta, and investigate
thoroughly the role of the latter in causing the disease.
Since toxemia was peculiar to pregnant women, I said,
the presence of the fetus and placenta must have something to do with the cause of the disease.

I outlined to the group the various approaches and the
different experimental procedures for investigating
these problems, including the approximate length of
time for each investigation and the personnel and equipment needed. When I finished, Dr. Ferris said, "This is
at least a five-year project."

"Maybe," I replied, "but if we all work together we
might start making major contributions within six
months." Everyone was excited.

To augment the funds that Ferris had from the university and from granting agencies, we received some financial assistance from various drug companies, which helped us to hire more research technicians. Our primary goal was to find answers to the following questions:

How is the blood pressure controlled during normal pregnancy, and are the mechanisms different from those of nonpregnant individuals?

How and by what mechanisms does blood pressure rise in toxemia?

Is lowering of the blood pressure in toxemia beneficial or detrimental to the patient's organs and tissues?

How does Veratrone act in lowering the blood pressure, and what are its active ingredients?

We thought that we needed at least two years to get valid answers to these questions, but by working hard and with enthusiasm we were able to do it in less than one. We found that the blood pressure of a normal pregnant woman was maintained by mechanisms that were entirely different from those of a nonpregnant individual. We further showed that the rise in blood pressure in toxemia was detrimental, and that it was caused by a narrowing of the small blood vessels that feed organs and tissues. This condition could be compared to a garden hose with a nozzle: when the nozzle is tightened, less water goes through the opening and the pressure in the hose goes up; but if the nozzle is open, the flow increases and the pressure in the hose falls. And this was exactly what Veratrone was doing: opening the nozzle.

These results and related findings were published in a series of papers in scientific journals. They produced a sharp reaction among obstetricians, since they went totally against established concepts. Dr. Eastman, of Johns Hopkins, was at that time just beginning to publish a new journal, called *Obstetrics and Gynecology Survey,* which summarized published reports in the field and commented on their importance. In commenting on our papers, he concluded that our research would open a new era in obstetrics that might revolutionize current thinking.

In fact, Eastman sent one of his brightest young assistants, Harry Prystowsky, to work with me for a year. The work we did together on the mechanisms that render the pregnant woman sensitive to spinal anesthesia established a landmark in the application of physiological research to obstetrics and had many ramifications in the fields of circulation and anesthesia. Prystowsky later became one of the leading investigators in obstetrics and chairman of the department at the University of Florida. He is now provost for Medical Sciences at the new Penn State University at Hershey, Pennsylvania.

While these activities were unfolding at a fast pace in studies of toxemia and blood-pressure regulation, I devoted what spare time I had to another important research problem. With the help of a resident, I designed an investigative project to record the magnitude of uterine contractions during labor. This had never been done before, but it was essential to our understanding of the mechanisms of labor and delivery at term or of premature babies. With an electroencephalographic machine that I had borrowed from the Department of Neurology, we made the first attempt to record uterine contraction. We selected a young black girl, pregnant for the first time and close to term gestation. We took her to the laboratory and had her recline in bed. We placed one of the pick-up electrodes on her abdomen above the uterus and clipped the other electrode to her uterine cervix through the vagina. We then turned the machine on and were thrilled to see on the rolling paper the first tracings of uterine activities ever recorded. The resident and I stepped out of the room for a moment to savor this extraordinary event and left the machine running. We had hardly reached the corridor when we heard the patient yelling, "Doctor! Doctor! Please hurry!" We rushed back, thinking that the patient might have had an electric shock due to a malfunctioning of the instruments. But when I reached her, she said, "Doctor, please—they're broadcasting from my womb!" For a moment I thought the patient had lost her mind. I leaned over and put my ear close to her vagina. Sure enough, I heard a sportscaster say, "Strike one!" The defective electroencephalographic machine had picked up radio interference from a baseball game of the Cincinnati Reds. The news about this amusing "research" incident spread rapidly over the campus. It was picked up by the wire services and appeared in various newspapers in America and abroad. The magazine *Medical Economics* conferred on me its annual award for "extraordinary events" in the practice of medicine. I must confess that the publicity created by this incident was to a certain extent most rewarding.

Because of the many research projects we were pursuing, we found that we needed more funds. We applied for a grant from the National Institutes of Health, the first ever received by that organization from an obstetrical department. It was quickly approved. For additional manpower, I turned to the resident staff and students. I organized their schedules in such a way as to allow all of them to participate in the research program. As an additional incentive I included their names as co-authors on the published reports.

My fellowship from the Institute of International Education expired at the end of 1946, and I was supposed to return to Brazil. But Garber and Ferris convinced the dean to promote me to assistant professor and urged me to stay in Cincinnati.

The research activities were advancing rapidly, and exciting new information on toxemia and the whole physiology of pregnancy was streaming in. In less than two years, the Department of Obstetrics of the University of Cincinnati was to become known as the site of the most original research in the field of obstetrics. Young doctors from all over the world who aspired to research and academic careers in obstetrics began applying for positions in the department. Medical societies in America and abroad—particularly those concerned with obstetrics—invited me, to speak to their members, and many of them conferred on me honorary membership.

Then, toward the end of 1947, unexpected events placed obstacles in the way of our research and teaching and almost sent me back to Brazil.

18 · Deportation Danger

MY first inkling that something was wrong came when I received a summons from the local draft board asking me to appear to discuss my situation.

I had a lengthy interview with the man in charge. "Have you ever served in the military?" he asked. I said that I had, for one year in Brazil. "I'm not talking about Brazil," he said. "I mean here in the United States." I told him that I did not know I was supposed to serve in the military here. "If you want me to," I said, "I'm ready to start now." He proceeded to ask questions and take notes on my life history, my work, my reasons for coming to the United States, and what I was doing now. He examined my passport and all my other documents. Then he asked me to return in a week.

I called Garber to tell him about this. There was a moment of silence. Then he gave me the impression, somewhat evasively, that I should not worry. I then told Ferris about it. "That's ridiculous," he said. "What the hell can you do in the military?" He promised to look into it.

When I returned to the draft board on the appointed day, I was received this time somewhat less harshly. "We went over your case," the head of the board said, "and we're in one hell of a dilemma. You're too old and too high in the academic world to be drafted as a private. And you can't serve as an officer because you aren't an American citizen. So go back to your work and keep in touch with us once a month." I thanked him and left, thinking that the problem had been solved.

Hardly two weeks had passed before I received several letters from the University of São Paulo and from professors who were friends of mine, all asking what was going on. They had received letters from a group of doctors in Cincinnati inquiring whether it was true that I had gone to the medical school, that I was a doctor, and that I had training in obstetrics and gynecology. This group wanted official documents for confirmation.

It is very difficult to describe my reaction to this news even now, nearly thirty years later. I sat with the letters in front of me, completely stunned and unable to articulate my thoughts. Here on the one hand I had letters from major universities around the world praising my research work and asking if they could send their bright young men to work with me; and on the other hand I had letters sent to my university by doctors asking if I were a charlatan. I felt outraged and betrayed. My diploma hung on the wall in my office, and had been seen by people at the Institute of International Education as well as at the several universities I had visited, including the University of Cincinnati.

With these letters from Brazil, several things that had happened to me during the past six months became clear. I had applied for membership in two medical societies, the membership of which was limited to obstetrical/gynecological men in the Midwest, but my applications had been consistently turned down, even though by that time I was an honorary member of several national and international societies. I was to learn later that some doctors in Cincinnati had blackballed me. Furthermore, when I applied to take the exam for the Specialty Board of Obstetrics and Gynecology, my application was turned down without a word of explanation.

I called Garber and asked him if he could meet with me as soon as possible.

"Is it the draft board again?" he asked.

"No," I said, "it's worse."

When I discussed the letters from Brazil, he finally told me the truth. Some doctors on the staff and others in the community had been after him to fire me. They were angry with me for the changes I had introduced into the department and the charges I had brought up about unnecessary surgery. Garber said, "I have resisted all their demands and have refused to fire you because of the important work you've been doing in teaching, research, and patient care." After more talk, he said, "Why don't you ask your university in Brazil to comply with their demands? You have nothing to hide. You know, this is a conservative town. They don't like foreigners much. I don't know what they'll do next."

After this conversation I was more concerned than assured. I knew Garber was not a very strong chairman, but I thought this stemmed from the fact that he was not being paid and had no firm obligations toward the university. Later I learned that Garber did not want to antagonize the doctors. Many thought he took the chairmanship to increase his own practice and not to benefit the university. I also learned later that part of the doctors' hostility toward me was indirectly aimed at Garber. To them, I was making an international name for the department, thereby raising Garber's prestige, and they resented this.

In view of Garber's equivocation, I thought I had better start making preparations to leave. I decided to discuss the matter first with Ferris, who always welcomed

me with his cheerful attitude and hardy optimism. The
letters from Brazil were in Portuguese, so he could not
read them; I summarized their contents. "The bastards!"
he said. "How low can they get?" He asked me what I
was going to do. I told him about my conversation with
Garber and how discouraged I was; I said that I was
getting ready to leave for Brazil.

Ferris exploded. "The hell you are! You can't let those
sons of bitches win! You're doing some of the most out-
standing work in the country—probably in the world.
You can't abandon all this because of a bunch of ig-
noramuses who don't know any better. Don't do a
damned thing. I'll talk to the dean about it." And before
I could answer, he was gone.

The news spread quickly among the science faculty.
Many were outraged and rallied to my support. Several
went to the dean and protested strongly. The dean called
me to his office a couple of days later. He began by
complimenting me on what I had been doing in the
department, not only in research but also in teaching and
in patient care. "I have heard nothing but praise from
the regular faculty," he said. "As for that business with
the clinicians," he continued, "don't do anything about
it. Write your university to ignore their letters. I have
here everything they want; I'll talk to them."

I thanked him and left his office. I wrote to São Paulo
and told them to ignore the letters and went back to
work as if nothing had happened. I dropped the idea of
applying for membership in any obstetrical and gynecological societies in the Midwest, but did something else
instead. One of the societies that had turned me down—
the Central Association of Obstetricians and Gynecologists—announced a prize award for the best research
paper submitted each year by members or nonmembers.
So I entered one entitled "Mechanisms of Blood Pres-

sure Maintenance in Normal and Toxemic Pregnancies." It was a piece of original work and I was sure it would impress the committee in charge of selection. Sure enough, a month later I was told that my paper had been chosen; I was to deliver it before the annual meeting of the association.

On the day of the meeting I presented slides of the data but did not read from my manuscript. I had rehearsed the presentation for days before the meeting—a system that I adopted for the rest of my academic career. At the end of my presentation I received a standing ovation. Unfortunately, none of the antagonistic Cincinnati doctors was there. But the president of the association came to me and said, "Nick, I feel ashamed now for the society's action in turning you down. But we couldn't do anything about it—the opposition was from your own group."

When three or four months had passed since my conversation with the dean, and I had heard nothing, I assumed he had talked to that group and they had decided to drop the matter. In this I was mistaken. It was just the calm before the storm. A hurricane was to whip me and leave me hanging and twisting in the wind for the next three years.

I received a letter from the Immigration and Naturalization Service in Cincinnati, summoning me to review my visa status with them. I went on the appointed day and was received by the head of the office. In his physical appearance, his stern attitude, and his manner of speaking, he resembled very much the late Charles Laughton in his role of the detective Javert in the movie *Les Misérables*.

"News has reached us that you're receiving a monthly salary of about a hundred and fifty dollars. Is that true?" he asked.

I replied, "I'm receiving the sum of two hundred dollars a month as a stipend from the university."

"You know that you're violating the terms of your visa, don't you?" he said.

"No, I didn't know that. In fact, I had no idea that there were different types of visas."

He proceeded to give me a lengthy explanation of the different types of visas and what each one would permit a person to do. He wound up by saying: "You entered the United States on a visitor's visa, which doesn't permit you to do any work for income purposes." Then he exploded the bomb: "You are now subject to deportation from this country. Legal proceedings will be immediately initiated in this office against you, unless you volunteer to leave this country of your own will within the next seven to ten days."

I tried to explain to him the importance of what I was doing, not only for myself but also for the university as well as all mankind. It was futile.

What is the purpose of this struggle? I asked myself. Certainly I was helping save the lives of a few mothers and babies, but thousands upon thousands of them were dying all over the world every day from disease, starvation, wars that they had nothing to do with. Then I remembered my father's last words before his death: "Sometimes you'd rather admire a dog than a man!"

I was depressed when I reached the hospital. I called Garber and told him what had happened. His advice was to get a lawyer; he gave me the names of some friends of his. I called one of them and he told me about his fee. I couldn't possibly afford it.

The following day I asked Ferris for advice. He was distressed. "We've got to fight them, Nick," he said.

"I've had enough fighting," I answered. "I don't want any more. Besides, it'll do no good."

"Don't give me that again," he said. "You've fought against much worse, like the French and the Senegalese. Here at least we have a democracy with the right to appeal!" He persuaded me to keep on working and fight it out.

Our group was just then on the verge of an important breakthrough in our research on pregnant women. A new method had been developed at the University of Pennsylvania to measure blood flow to the brain, using nitrous oxide. I had adapted this method to measure the blood flow to the pregnant uterus in normal and toxemic pregnancies. This would determine why so many babies died in the uterus in toxemia. We were to show later that the transfer of most of the essential and vital elements from the mother to the fetus depends on the rate of blood flow. This discovery was to be cited among the accomplishments that earned me the Virginia Apgar Award thirty years later.

After a great deal of soul-searching, I decided that I could not abandon this work now, and I would therefore fight the Immigration authorities without a lawyer. I made a list of all the work I was doing in research, teaching, and patient care. To this I added testimonial letters from Garber, Ferris, and the dean. I took the whole thing to the Immigration Office head and told him that I could not possibly leave the United States at this stage. He accepted the documents and said, "You'll hear from us."

A month or so later I heard from them: an official order for deportation. Since I had no previous criminal record and was engaged in worthy work at the university, I was allowed to depart voluntarily within a month. I decided to appeal. I had found a lawyer who was teaching at the university and who volunteered to help me without pay. We prepared an appeal, to which we attached statements from professors, the dean, residents, and students. The appeal was filed and I returned to my work.

One day four or five months later, when I had just finished making ward rounds with the residents and was about to enter a classroom to lecture to the senior class, the department's secretary came up to me and said that there was a U.S. marshal in the office. There, without any formality, he handed me a document stating that the appeal had been rejected and my immediate deportation was ordered. But, he added, if you sign this document promising the United States government to depart voluntarily, we will let you go on your own.

I told him that I was late for my class and asked if he could wait for my decision until I finished my lecture. He said yes and followed me to the lecture hall, though he remained outside. I gave what I thought would be my last lecture at the university. It was one of the most dramatic I had ever delivered. I ended by saying, "Now I leave you, probably forever. I came here with many hopes and a burning desire to carry out the best teaching, research, and patient-care program that I could manage. My efforts have been rewarded by worldwide recognition for this department. But events beyond my control have forced me to abandon this program. In the corridor outside this classroom, a U.S. marshal is waiting with an order to deport me from this country, because I made the error of accepting two hundred dollars a month as a stipend. My appeals have been turned down. All that I can say now is good-bye and good luck."

Applause followed, with a lot of shouting: "No! No!" "Stay!" "Let's march on the dean's office!" I left the classroom, signed the paper, and told the marshal I would leave within ten days. Meanwhile, the senior class went to the dean's office and asked him to stop my deportation.

A week later I went around and said good-bye to my friends at the university. I rejected all of their appeals to "stay on and fight it out." I then took the train to New York, where I was to report to the Immigration Office before leaving. When I told them the boat would not leave for another week, they asked me to report to the office every day. They would send a man to see me off on the ship when it was ready to sail.

While I was waiting in New York, I visited several friends who were working at different universities. I learned that the students, the house staff, and various faculty members of the University of Cincinnati had made another forceful demand for action by the dean and the university president. Senator Robert Taft had been requested to use his power to stop my deportation.

Apparently, Taft and other Ohio congressmen presented the case to President Truman. The day before I was to board the ship for Brazil, I went as usual to the Immigration Office. The information clerk told me that the director wanted to see me. He received me graciously and told me that he had a message from the Justice Department in Washington saying that the President of the United States had suspended the deportation order. "If you want to return to your job in Cincinnati, we will be happy to make arrangements at the government's expense. Your case will be reopened and further hearings will be conducted in Cincinnati and Detroit."

I was overwhelmed with joy and gratitude for the loyalty of students and faculty. I returned to Cincinnati and was welcomed warmly by everyone.

Two days later I reported to the Immigration Office. I was surprised at the friendliness this time. I was told to go back to my usual duties; my case would be reopened, but from now on would be handled by the Regional Office in Detroit.

19 · A New Family

MY research work was increasing rapidly, as was the teaching and patient-care load. Because after my return to the University of Cincinnati I felt a degree of security, albeit temporary, I began accepting research fellows from various parts of the United States and from abroad. These fellows helped not only in research but also in teaching and patient care. Their presence filled the gap left by the clinicians, who had all but ceased to show up for their assignments.

Meanwhile, I had grown tired of living with the residents in a room in the basement of the hospital. There was very little freedom, and I was constantly interrupted in my studies or awakened at night by the phone calls to the residents. I decided to move into a small one-room apartment near the hospital.

I was also lonely and tired of cooking my own food and washing my own clothes. It was natural that the idea of marriage would cross my mind.

During the early years in Cincinnati, I had occasionally visited my sister and her husband in Detroit. They were a retired couple and owned some real estate. Now and then they took me to Toledo, Ohio, where there was a large Lebanese colony. I was introduced to various Lebanese friends.

On one of those visits I met Pauline. She was born in

America, but her parents, the Hannas, were from a town in Lebanon not too distant from Rachaya. They had known my father, having met him on his various tours to recruit revolutionaries.

Pauline was three years younger than I and lived with her family in Toledo. At the time of our first meeting, she was working as a manager of a drugstore.

Our friendship developed slowly. During the first year, I saw her only while passing through Toledo on my way to Detroit. Yet when my problems with the Immigration Service became serious, she came down to Cincinnati and offered to help in any way she could. She gave me much encouragement and urged me not to leave the United States. Our relationship deepened, and in 1948 we decided to get married.

I have always hated ceremonial weddings and pompous funerals. Pauline's family wanted a big wedding, to impress their friends. I refused and told Pauline that if she wanted to marry me, it had to be a simple ceremony without relatives or parents. She agreed, and we met in Buffalo. She came with a woman friend, who would serve as a witness. I did not have a witness. So I went out to the street and found a man selling newspapers. I bought a newspaper, told him my story, and asked him if he would witness my wedding. He did, and the civil wedding was completed in less than five minutes.

Later, Pauline persuaded me to have a religious ceremony for the sake of her family. Although I did not believe in it, I agreed. We went to a Catholic church and talked with the priest. He asked me innumerable questions and talked about Catholics and their responsibilities toward the church and its beliefs. One question made me furious. He asked, "Do you believe in abortion?"

I said, "Yes."

He said, "This is contrary to the Catholic religion. If you want to be married here, you must promise God that you will never practice it."

I lost my temper and told him, almost shouting, "I didn't struggle to study medicine for all those years so you or anyone like you could tell me how to practice it! In medicine I do whatever I consider best for the patient. I don't need your endorsement of our marriage!" I looked at Pauline, grabbed her hand, and said, "Let's go!" And that was the end of the religious ceremony.

We returned to the one-room apartment in Cincinnati, but it was too small for a married couple. My stipend from the university had by then increased, and the National Institutes of Health allowed me to allocate a certain portion of my grant as a salary. I thought that this amount would allow us to move to a somewhat bigger apartment. Such a move became more necessary when I received news that my mother was coming to visit me, determined to take me back to Brazil. She had heard that I was having problems with Immigration and had become very upset.

Hardly had we moved into a new apartment when I received news from Detroit to appear for hearings on my immigration status. With my marriage to an American citizen, the whole problem had acquired a new aspect. Pauline now joined me in the struggle to remain in the United States. The Immigration authorities first thought that I had gotten married in order to prevent them from deporting me. They began investigating the background of the marriage, particularly how long I had known Pauline, but they could not find any evidence that the marriage was for the purpose of circumventing the law.

At the first hearing, when I saw my file on the desk of the officer in charge of the Regional Office, I was flabbergasted at how huge it had become. The officer asked if I had a lawyer representing me. I said, "No, I can't afford one." Then the questioning began. It went over the same grounds gone over before, but this time it was more thorough and more sympathetic to my position. After they finished with me, they started questioning Pauline. Altogether, we stayed about three hours. Finally they told us to go home; we would hear from them later. I got busy again with my work, and Pauline spent her time furnishing the apartment and making a comfortable home for us.

Shortly after the hearing, I heard from friends that investigators from the Justice Department had been asking questions. I told my friends not to hide anything, to tell the truth.

My mother arrived in America, but decided to visit my sister in Canada first. After staying a couple of weeks there, my mother visited my other sister in Detroit and asked me to meet her there. Our reunion was emotional. We had not seen each other for four years. I gave her a short account of my troubles and told her not to worry. As I expected, she was angry. "What are you wasting your time here for? Your colleagues in Brazil are becoming millionaires and you're working here, killing yourself for nothing! What are you going to get from all this research and from saving a few women and babies? Look what you get as a reward—a real kick in the ass from the government!"

My mother stayed for about four months, trying always to convince me to return with her and make a fortune in Brazil. I had never had a vacation since coming to the States, so I thought I would go back with her to see what the academic situation was at the University of São Paulo. But while in New York attending the International Congress of Obstetrics and Gynecology, I bumped into Professor Raul Briquet, the chairman of the

Obstetrics Department, and Professor José Medina, the chairman of Gynecology, from the University of São Paulo. They said that they had been reading my research reports and were proud of me. They were honest and also told me that in Brazil there was no money, space, equipment, or positions to do this kind of research. They advised me to stay where I was if I was still interested in research. But if I wanted to practice and make money, São Paulo was just as good as anyplace else. I was somewhat disturbed by this talk, but made no immediate decision. What made me decide not to return at this time was the news from the Immigration Service that a decision on my case was about to be rendered and I should be in this country to hear it.

Three days later I put my mother on a plane, and she returned to Brazil alone. There is no point in describing how she felt about it.

Shortly after New Year's of 1950 good news came. First, I received a letter from the Justice Department stating that the order of deportation against me had been permanently canceled; I had been given a permanent residency visa and would be eligible for U.S. citizenship upon completing five years of residency in the United States. Next, I received word from the dean's office that I had been promoted to associate professor of obstetrics, with a substantial increase in salary, which could also be supplemented by a certain amount from my research grant. That same month the NIH approved a large research grant, which permitted us to hire more technicians and fellows.

Amid all this came one sad occurrence: Gene Ferris decided to leave the University of Cincinnati to become chairman of internal medicine at Emory University, in Atlanta, and he took with him a number of assistants who had been collaborating with me. With the dean's acquiescence, he was kind enough to turn over to me all the laboratory and office space that he had occupied for so many years. This was the best news of all, since I could then set up my own laboratories and run things my own way. When Ferris came to say good-bye, I burst into tears. It must have been a premonition. In Atlanta, Ferris suffered from the same difficulties with his colleagues that I had had. After struggling for two years, he left Atlanta and died in New York of a heart attack in 1953.

Our research activities, and the stream of scientific reports that appeared in professional journals, had made the Department of Obstetrics in Cincinnati the mecca of investigators in the field of obstetrics. Visitors from all major universities in the United States as well as from other countries always stopped in Cincinnati now to see what was going on. These visits brought close friendships with many research workers in obstetrics the world over. These contacts also brought many honors and recognition to me and my co-workers. At the same time, speaking invitations came from various medical societies, hospital staffs, and other organizations. I found them rewarding because they brought more people to work with our team, and consequently more grants.

In the autumn of 1950 Pauline and I decided to visit Brazil to see my family and friends. When we arrived at the airport of São Paulo, a huge crowd was waiting for us. Again my mother mobilized everyone to pressure me to remain in Brazil, but to no avail. During my stay I gave a series of lectures at the departments of obstetrics of the universities of São Paulo and Rio.

I also saw my son, Robin, who had been living with his mother and had grown to be a handsome boy of eight. His mother had married by now and had several other children. Pauline and I asked her to let Robin come with us to the United States, where he would have a better future. After some hesitation, she agreed.

I returned to the United States, while Pauline remained in Brazil a little longer to take care of Robin's papers. When they rejoined me, about two weeks later, they did so at a beautiful house that I had rented for a year in one of the nicest suburbs of Cincinnati. It was a pleasant surprise for both of them. A year later we bought our own house in the same neighborhood. It was the first house I had ever owned in my life.

In 1951, I was given my U.S. citizenship at the courthouse in Cincinnati.

20 · The Society for Gynecologic Investigation

PRIOR to 1947 the specialty of obstetrics and gynecology had been a conservative branch of medicine with little basic research, if any. Most of the departments were run by part-time faculty members who were often busy with private practices. These conservative individuals dominated the obstetrical and gynecological societies. Their scientific programs were largely devoted to reporting clinical problems and statistical data. Their discussions were usually pompous, dull, and full of mutual praise. The membership was limited, and even young men with good research backgrounds had a hard time getting in.

The introduction of basic research into the specialty created a new generation eager to pursue academic careers in the field. Many universities demanded that obstetrics and gynecology chairmen and faculty members have research and academic training. In addition, the federal government, which in the past had paid lip service to this specialty, began a program to improve its scientific status. Liberal grants became available through the National Institutes of Health, the Children's Bureau, and other agencies, and by 1950 the number of young investigators and academic career men in obstetrics and gynecology had increased substantially. Toward the middle of 1950, I became convinced that a new society was needed where these young investigators could pre-

sent their work. I saw it as a dynamic young society—
and one that would remain so—where a presentation
could be thoroughly discussed and dissected. Such an
organization would serve as a forum to educate the
young researcher and show him not only the good points
of his data but also the deficiencies.

But how does one organize a new society without antagonizing the "old guard"? First, I wrote to younger
members of the established societies, but most of them
answered that there were plenty of societies already.

Discouraged by their response, I decided to change my
strategy. Aware that research on toxemia had generated
a great deal of interest and excitement, I proposed a
debate on research in hypertension in general and toxemia of pregnancy in particular. I decided to discuss the
matter with William Dieckman, of the University of
Chicago. He was most enthusiastic and offered to write
personal letters to a dozen people urging them to join the
group. Some of the answers were favorable, others luke-
warm.

Early in 1951 the American College of Obstetrics and
Gynecology met in Cincinnati. Most of the people
Dieckman and I had been in touch with attended. I invited twelve of them to a dinner at the University Club
and brought up the subject of forming a new society.
Dieckman spoke in favor of such an organization, and all
those present agreed to join. Dieckman designated a date
for officially forming the society. Later a list of founding
members was drawn up, and much debate and argument
followed regarding the name of the organization, its ob-
jectives, and the qualifications for membership.

At a meeting in Chicago a few months later, the name
"Society of University Gynecologists" was adopted,
over my strenuous objections. I thought this name snob-
bish and felt that it implied exclusion of investigators

who were not members of university faculties. Nevertheless, I went along with the majority in order to get things moving. Dieckman was elected the first president, and Lou Hellman secretary.

At my urging, the name was later changed to "Society for Gynecologic Investigation." And I was elected its third president, in 1955.

The society now is the pride of the obstetrical and gynecological specialty. Its membership rose from fifteen in 1951 to several hundred in 1978. To this day it remains the society of the "Young Turks"—the youthful investigators in the field—offering the greatest stimuli to research and academic careers in obstetrics and gynecology. For me, it represents the greatest achievement of my life.

Part Four

CALIFORNIA

21 · The Fight to Go West

IN the middle of 1951 I received from various universities offers of positions in their departments of obstetrics and gynecology. I also received offers of private practice, which I rejected promptly; private practice, as I had seen it conducted in both Brazil and the United States, did not appeal to me.

One particular offer that did appeal to me came from the University of Chicago, where William Dieckman was the chairman of the Department of Obstetrics and Gynecology. We had grown close during our efforts to organize the Society for Gynecologic Investigation. He was interested in my work on the toxemia of pregnancy, particularly in the technique I had developed for measuring the rate of the blood flow to the pregnant uterus. At his invitation, in the summer of 1951 I delivered a lecture to his department. After the lecture he offered me an associate professorship, with tenure, which I did not have in Cincinnati. The salary was also higher, and I would have benefits, research support, and space. One disadvantage was that there were two heads of the department, Dieckman and M. Edward Davis, who rotated every year or so. This resulted in a great deal of friction and hostility among the staff members. I promised Dieckman I would think about the offer and give him an answer in a few weeks.

Before I had time to consider the Chicago offer, however, Dr. Daniel Morton, chairman of the newly developed Medical School of the University of California at Los Angeles, visited us unexpectedly in Cincinnati.

Pauline and I liked Dan and Lila Morton immediately, and by the time they left, it was as though we had known them for years; we were already bound by warm, and lasting, ties. I was most impressed by the simplicity and gentlemanly quality of the man.

While Pauline took Lila shopping, Dan explained to me the purpose of his visit. "Nowadays any department in a medical school needs a dynamic research program," he said. "It's a stimulus for the faculty, house staff, and students. I don't know anything about research, but I appreciate its importance. I've been looking around for the last few months, and most people agree that you are the man to start a research program in a new medical school."

I was extremely flattered by what he said. We discussed the details of such a job and the rank. He explained that the University of California was a state-supported institution and that appointments required a lot of red tape. "As chairman," he said, "I can submit your name only for a rank of associate professor, step three or four. That means you'd be eligible for promotion to full professor within one or two years. But let me make it clear: I can only propose; it's up to the ad-hoc committee, the dean, the budget committee, the chancellor, and finally the regents to accept or turn down my request." Then he added: "You know those regents are a very conservative bunch. They are mostly wealthy businessmen. They screen candidates for tenure positions very thoroughly."

I felt so taken with the sincerity and humility of this man that I would have accepted a job as an orderly had he offered it to me. "I understand," I said. "I'd love to work with you. You can count on me to help you build one of the finest departments in the country." We left it at that. He took my curriculum vitae and all the necessary papers with him.

One thing Morton did not tell me about the appointment at the University of California was that the regents and the various committees would require letters from prominent individuals supporting my appointment. This unintentional omission on Dan's part was to cause me much anxiety over the next eighteen months.

The news of the offer from UCLA spread fast among both my friends and my foes in Cincinnati. Some of my friends on the faculty tried to persuade me to remain in Cincinnati, but I had made up my mind. All I needed was the official offer from Morton, bearing the regents' approval. I waited and waited, for weeks and months. Finally I wrote to Ernie Page, of the University of California at San Francisco, who had suggested my name to Morton, and asked him if he knew the reason for the delay. He said he had some ideas, but for the moment preferred not to elaborate.

A few months before Morton offered me the UCLA job, I had received an invitation from the Southern California Assembly of Obstetrics and Gynecology to be a guest speaker during their 1952 meeting in February.

The audience was composed of about four hundred highly qualified specialists. I was the youngest of five speakers and of course I planned my "show" carefully because I knew I was being assessed by the UCLA group.

Dan and Lila Morton invited us to meet Jerry Moore, his second in command, and other members of the faculty after the meeting. When I was able to speak to Dan alone, I asked him about the delay in my appointment. After a slight hesitation he told me that the regents had received several unfavorable letters from doctors in Cincinnati, some of which had stated that I was a Communist. "The regents are very conservative and hesitate to offer a tenure position to someone controversial," he told me again. "I've tried my best to change their minds and have obtained letters from people outside Cincinnati. I want you here badly. Give me time and I'll see what I can do." Again I was overcome by the sincerity of the man. I promised to wait for his answer and not accept any other offer.

When I returned to Cincinnati, I told the story to friends in the basic-sciences departments. They were outraged. Although in the past they had opposed my leaving, now they were determined to see me get the UCLA job. Consequently, Roger Crafts and William Atkinson from Anatomy, George Acheson from Pharmacology, and William Lotspeich from Physiology wrote strong letters recommending me for the job.

Six months later came the official letter from Morton. All he could get from the regents was an appointment as a "Visiting Associate Professor" for two years. If my behavior was satisfactory during the two years' probation, I would be given tenure and would be eligible for promotion to full professor. Although I felt the "visiting" label a little embarrassing, I accepted the offer for the beginning of the 1953 academic year.

We sold our house in Cincinnati and left by car in early August. I had mixed feelings as we drove out of Cincinnati. After all, I owed something to the place. Eight years before, I had arrived, unknown. There had been problems in Cincinnati, but also many rewarding experiences. Enemies had tried to destroy me, but many close, sincere friends had given me all the support they could.

One last, disturbing incident occurred just before I

left my office at Cincinnati General Hospital. As I was packing my research files and books, Stan Garber appeared unexpectedly. I thought he had come to express his regrets about my leaving. Instead, he said, "Nick, you're free to take some of the papers and data books with you, but the slides that have been made here should remain here."

"Stan," I said, "these are my teaching slides, made from the data that I generated from my own research and paid for from my own grant. Why shouldn't I have the right to take them with me? I'd be glad to order a duplicate set for you." He wouldn't hear of it.

The argument grew worse when I told him I planned to take a few ampules of Inulin with me. Inulin was a substance used in research on the function of the kidneys. At that time, the raw material used to make it was imported from Hungary. Because of the Cold War with Russia, Inulin had become extremely scarce in the United States. I had purchased a substantial supply with my own grant and had more than five hundred ampules in the laboratory, because during that year my associates and I were working actively on kidney functions and their relation to toxemia. I knew that no one in the Department of Obstetrics would use this material after my departure and it would deteriorate. When I mentioned that I was taking a few ampules, Garber was very upset. He asked someone to make an inventory of the stock and said he wanted it to remain intact.

I dropped the idea of taking the Inulin; but after he left, I did take the most important slides I needed for teaching. After I had been in California six months, Garber found out about the missing slides. He wrote to Morton that I had stolen "university property." When Dan learned what was at stake, he laughed in amazement.

22 · Research at UCLA

WE arrived in Los Angeles and rented an apartment near the university. Shortly thereafter Dan and Lila Morton gave a reception to introduce us to the UCLA faculty.

The Medical School, with its many departments and research laboratories, was housed at that time in wooden barracks dispersed in various locations in Westwood. The Department of Obstetrics and Gynecology was located in a small room in one of these barracks that also served as the chairman's office; the departmental secretary worked in an adjoining cubicle. Jerry Moore had used a small area as a laboratory for tissue cultures. Clinical teaching was done at Harbor County General Hospital and St. John's Hospital, since UCLA did not have its own.

A few days after our arrival, Morton and I went to Dean Stafford Warren to see what space I could have for a research laboratory and an office. After a long search, we found a room in a barracks located on Wilshire Boulevard. I quickly transformed it into a comfortable laboratory for animal research. But for research on human subjects I had to go to Harbor County General Hospital, which was in Torrance, about twenty-five miles south of the Westwood campus. Harbor, like Cincinnati General Hospital, cared for indigent patients, who could be used for research. The hospital itself was composed of barracks placed side by side or interconnecting, over a huge area. Each medical department had from two to four barracks serving as wards. The Department of Obstetrics and Gynecology had four wards and another area for labor rooms and a delivery suite. The research laboratories at Harbor were located in another series of barracks, separated from those serving as hospital wards.

I was able to obtain one full barrack for my own human-research laboratories. It was not bad at all, having more than twice the space I had had in Cincinnati. Here again, with the aid of the NIH grants given me in Cincinnati and now transferred to UCLA, I was able to install a good human-research laboratory, well equipped with beds, so that pregnant patients could be brought in for examination. Adjoining this space were two rooms with facilities for complete blood and urine analyses, for research on kidney and cardiovascular functions.

I have always felt that the team approach to research is the best, and I therefore sought and established collaboration with other departments, particularly those of the basic sciences. This collaboration eventually led to the creation of multidisciplinary training programs for scientists in the field of reproductive biology.

Just before I left Cincinnati, I had begun to work on a project concerned with the study of the functions of the placenta and the fetus, and their contribution to the cause of toxemia. Among the hypotheses advanced was one postulating that the placental tissues in toxemia are ischemic (anemic) because of insufficient blood flow; under these circumstances they would produce a hormone or some other substance that caused the disease and constricted blood vessels in the whole body. Since at that time the hormone ACTH was in vogue in medical research, we decided to see if the placental tissues produced it. We worked on this project in collaboration with the scientific-research department of Armour Laboratories, in Chicago. At that time they had an excellent method for isolating ACTH from tissues: human placentas were obtained from women after delivery, drained of all blood, and frozen. They were then shipped by air in dry ice to Chicago. At Armour, the placental tissue was purified and reduced to a small amount of powder, which could be tested in rats for ACTH activities.

After I moved to California, I continued shipping placentas to Chicago. When the purified powder arrived from Armour Laboratories, I needed the special breed of hypophysectomized rats (animals whose pituitary glands had been removed) for testing the powder. In the barracks at UCLA I did not have the facilities to produce this special breed of rat. Fortunately, at that time a new animal supplier opened facilities in Chicago to supply scientists with the rats already operated on for pituitary ablation. I signed a contract with him for a certain number of these animals to be shipped to me by air every week. Because of the loss of their pituitary gland, these rats were fragile and had to be used immediately upon arrival. Since in those days flights between Los Angeles and Chicago took a long time, the rats usually arrived at the Los Angeles airport after 4:00 P.M., and often after 10:00 P.M. My technician and I would work on them almost all night, then take the following morning off to sleep.

Despite this difficult schedule, the project was successful. We were the first group of scientists to show that the human placenta does indeed produce ACTH-like substances. This discovery had an enormous impact on later research related to the production of other hormones by the placenta. It also gave us the first clue as to the importance of the placenta to fetal life and to the complexity of its functions. This led us into research for the next twenty years on the many fascinating aspects of intrauterine life and the adaptation of the infant to the external environment after birth.

In the area of human research, I continued work on the various physiological changes in the pregnant organism and how these changes are altered by disease. Of particular interest were the mechanisms by which pregnant women accumulate salt and water in the body, which leads to edema. The role of the kidneys in such cases was intensively investigated, as were the influences of the standing and supine positions on the cardiovascular and renal functions of the pregnant woman throughout gestation.

Several residents, fellows, and faculty members collaborated in these studies. The results pointed out decisively that a pregnant organism could not be judged by the standards of a nonpregnant one, either in health or when diseased. Numerous modifications are introduced by pregnancy which to the unaware person may appear to be pathologic states.

In the 1950s the pharmaceutical industry came out with a new drug for high blood pressure and one for edema removal practically every year. Our team took an active part in testing many of these drugs, and in standardizing their use in pregnant women with diseases related to pregnancy. Reports on this part of our research, written by members of the house staff and faculty, appeared in various medical journals.

Between 1954 and 1955 the university's new Health Sciences Center, containing hospital and research facilities, was completed. I was assigned a spacious office, a secretarial office, and a series of laboratories for biochemical research. With a liberal grant from the NIH for modernizing and equipping the laboratories with the latest research tools, we became a well-organized team, functioning at top speed within six months.

On the personal front, I had bought a lot on Amalfi Drive and began building a house of my own. Our architect, Randy Head, had been forced into exile in Yugoslavia for three years during the Joseph McCarthy investigations and had just returned to the States. He put all his imagination and energy into building us an attractive house at moderate cost. We moved in, but had no funds left to furnish the house. We thought of selling even before the landscaping was done, but decided, for one thing, to use the old furniture. The architect generously postponed collecting his fees and convinced the builder to accept payment in small monthly installments. We did have to buy new draperies, because the house had a lot of glass, and for that I borrowed money from friends. The wife of a colleague at UCLA and the architect drew some plans for landscaping for virtually no fee. And with the help of Robin, friends, and the husbands of some grateful patients, we did the planting ourselves. So we were able to keep the house, and we still live there.

The human-research laboratories had now moved completely from Harbor to the UCLA hospital, and doctors throughout the Los Angeles and Orange County area, and from as far away as Bakersfield and Santa Barbara, began referring their complicated cases, particularly those with toxemia, to our team. Within a year of its opening, the UCLA hospital had an unusually large percentage of complicated obstetrical cases. This increase further stimulated our research, not only on obstetrical complications but also on the physiology and biochemistry of the mother and her fetus in the normal state. Numerous questions came up: What effects do contractions of the pregnant uterus have on the body functions of the mother and on the transfer of substances to the fetus through the placenta? What factors are responsible for initiating labor at the correct mature date? What causes premature birth? What are the functions of the amniotic fluid surrounding the fetus, and what is this fluid's origin? Why do some infants born at term to healthy mothers appear depressed and of abnormal color? What are the effects of anesthesia on both mother and baby? What causes the blue-baby disease?

As these formidable questions erupted in rapid succession, several problems emerged that seemed almost insurmountable. The first one had ethical, moral, and legal implications, involving the limitation imposed on research performed on human subjects, particularly on pregnant women. Here two lives are involved—the life of the mother and that her child. Therefore an animal model had to be found whose vital functions were as close to the human body's as possible. In animals, pregnant or not, research could proceed far beyond the point allowed in humans. Moreover, a much larger number of experiments could be performed, thereby increasing the statistical validity of the information gained.

A second major problem related to methodology and instrumentation, particularly those concerned with the amount of blood flowing into an organ per unit of time. All past research pointed out with increasing clarity that the blood flow to an organ was one of the most important influences on the functioning of that organ. In the case of the pregnant uterus and the fetus, knowledge of the blood flow seemed essential if we were to provide a valid answer to the questions raised. In Cincinnati I had developed a method to measure the blood flow to the pregnant uterus by using nitrous oxide. But that method was technically complicated and its margin of error high. So we decided to search for a new one. Shortly before leaving

Cincinnati, I had come across a report that originated from the University of Chicago, describing an attempt to use an electromagnetic method for measuring the flow of blood in the whole animal or in individual organs. The electromagnetic method was more than a century old; the English physicist Michael Faraday had described it for the first time. That report, however, was the first attempt to apply the Faraday principle to the flow of blood in living organisms.

On one of my visits to the University of Chicago I had asked William Dieckman if he knew anything about the method. He had given me a discouraging answer. Yes, he replied, he had seen the report and had discussed it with one of its authors. The method was clumsy and crude, because the whole animal had to be placed between two huge magnets to get the flow signal. The meaning of that signal was totally unclear. He concluded: "The method can never be applied to human subjects or even to small blood vessels in animals. It will never amount to much." I took his word for it.

Yet the day my team and I debated how to start our search for a new technique to measure the rate of blood flow to organs, that report suddenly surfaced in my mind, and the picture of the two giant magnets flashed before my eyes. I rushed to the library, dug out the report, and reread it a half-dozen times. Finally I concluded that it might be possible to make those magnets smaller, and to make the instrumentation that picks up the signal more sensitive. In this way one might be able to use it on small blood vessels inside the animal's body.

Immediately I faced a major problem: I was not a physicist and knew nothing about designing instrumentation for such a project. We could send a man to Chicago to learn the method, but that would take a long time, and I was not prepared to wait. Furthermore, I had been told that the two scientists who published that report were no longer working together, and that the project had been abandoned. It seemed to me that the fastest way to accomplish what I wanted to do, and to get the correct information, was to get someone who had worked on the method to come to UCLA.

After an extensive search by myself, the chairman of the Biophysics Department, and the dean, a scientist by the name of Richard Tubovki, who was an expert in the field, was considered suitable for the position. I was authorized to inquire about him and make the first contact.

I decided to call three friends on the faculty of the university where this scientist worked who were acquainted with him and knew him personally. They were unanimous in their opinion: he was a genius, but an extremely difficult man to work with. One of my informants suggested that if we wanted him that much, we should hire him on a trial basis.

This struck me as the perfect solution, and that was what we did. We made the offer and Tubovki accepted and moved to UCLA in late 1955. Although his appointment was in biophysics, he was established in our animal-research laboratories. With the help of my NIH grants we were able to furnish a complete electronics laboratory and a workshop to build the necessary equipment for the flowmeter. Specialized engineering and electronics technicians were hired.

The initial goal was to make the blood-flow probe small enough to fit around vessels of very small size. At the same time, we had to build the amplifying instruments with enough sensitivity to record the flow signal as accurately as possible. Work on this project progressed satisfactorily throughout 1955 and 1956. In the spring of 1957, we had a flowmeter prototype ready for trial. We tested it on several anesthetized animals in the lab, and it worked well, although further improvement was necessary.

I persuaded the program committee of the Society for Gynecologic Investigation to let us make a demonstration of the flowmeter on a dog, without anesthesia, at its annual meeting in Los Angeles in April 1957. We implanted the flow probe around the artery supplying the head, using sterile technique. When the animal was ready, we sneaked it through the back door of the hotel into the meeting hall. The demonstration was successful and was hailed as one of the greatest innovations presented to a scientific meeting. It resulted in both prestige and further research grants.

23 · A Surprise Addition to the Family

IN June 1957, I received two letters from Brazil that caused me to interrupt my work for three weeks and that led to an event that was to give Pauline and me a great deal of joy.

One of the letters came from my younger brother Anis. He was getting married in September and wanted me to be his best man. The other letter was from the chief of gastroenterology at the University of São Paulo, Dr. José Fernandes Pontes. He had heard I was coming to Brazil and invited me to give a couple of lectures. I accepted both offers and flew to São Paulo in late August.

As usual, a big crowd of relatives and friends met me at the airport. At the age of seventy-five my mother was still energetic and full of determination. Her criticism was as biting as ever. The evenings at her house bored me, however, because the only topic of conversation was money. Practically all my relatives and friends asked how much I earned. I invariably exaggerated, so as to avoid my mother's scolding me for wasting time in America.

Three days before the wedding, which was set for a Saturday in September, I gave my first lecture at the university hospital. It was a summary of my current research on circulation and on the methods of measuring the various functions, particularly the rate of blood flow.

During the lecture several people in the audience were talking; I thought this unusual and indeed rude. At the end of the lecture, I overheard a group of obstetric and pediatric residents talking about an infant, a three-week-old boy, who had been found at the hospital door next to the trash cans. I asked one of the doctors if I could see the baby. Since Pauline and I had attempted to adopt a child in Los Angeles, without success, I thought it would not hurt to take a look at this poor abandoned child, who sooner or later would end up in some dilapidated orphanage.

The doctor led me to the nursery, and the head nurse escorted me to a crib where a baby lay with only his face showing. It was the custom in Brazil to swaddle a baby's whole body, including the arms and legs, to keep the limbs straight. I looked at the brown face and huge dark eyes and promptly fell in love.

I told the doctor and the head nurse in no uncertain terms, "This baby is going to be mine; I'm going to adopt it." They thought the baby lucky to find a home, particularly in the United States, and foresaw no problems with the hospital authorities or the Brazilian court. But they thought the American consul might cause difficulties.

I called Dr. Pontes and his wife and told them I had decided to adopt the baby. They were excited and said they had a lawyer friend who could get the adoption papers ready in less than two hours. Then I went home to tell my family. As I expected, my mother was up in arms. After all, I knew nothing about the child's mother and father, she said.

Meanwhile, Pauline, the prospective mother, was 7,000 miles away. I decided to bring the baby home as a surprise.

The next day, I went to see the American consul, an

austere, middle-aged gentleman whose face betrayed no hint of emotion. I told him the story of my falling in love with the abandoned baby and of my decision to adopt him.

"I hope you haven't started any adoption procedure yet," he said.

I answered, "No. But why shouldn't I?"

He gave me a long discourse on why I should not. He finished by saying, "He can't be admitted on your passport. And we can't get around the McCarran Act's requirement of an anti-Communist affidavit, even though he's still a baby. Furthermore, adoption procedures completed in Brazil are not recognized by American courts. So you might as well forget it."

I tried to persuade him to find some solution, but to no avail. I walked out of his office depressed and shaken. Just before I reached the elevator, someone tapped my shoulder. It was the consul's secretary. She motioned for me to follow her, and we went to an isolated spot behind the elevators.

"You want that baby badly, don't you?" she said. "I overheard your conversation with the consul. Listen to me now, and not a word about it to anyone. Promise?" I nodded and raised my fingers like a Boy Scout. "Adopt the baby," she advised. "Get him a Brazilian passport. Then bring the passport to me Monday afternoon, and I'll see that he gets the proper visa."

I asked if she was sure she knew what she was doing. "I don't want to adopt a baby and find out later that I can't get him into the States!"

"Either you have faith in me, or no baby," she said. "Look here, I'm an American citizen and I don't think admitting this baby will cause a calamity in the States."

I was overwhelmed. I dashed to the office of an old

friend and former classmate in night school who had become an important and influential lawyer. He immediately got to work. He called a judge to see if he would stay in court after 6:00 P.M. on Friday. He told the judge the reason. The judge said he had a commitment that evening, but added, "I'll hold court Saturday morning to hear this case."

On that morning, the lawyer, my brothers, Dr. Pontes, his wife, and I appeared in court. The judge made a short, moving speech about the baby's fortune in finding a nice home and a fine country. Then, just as he was signing the adoption papers, he looked up and said, "We have no name for this baby. What name would you like to give to him?"

I must have been in a daze. The only name that came to mind was that of my colleague and co-worker at UCLA, William Dignam. I said, "William, your honor." Mrs. Pontes added a middle name, Frederico, after one of her own boys whom I had known and liked. The ceremony ended with my name only appearing on the adoption documents. Thus I was the sole parent of a three-week-old son. Somehow, I said to myself, I'll manage to add Pauline's name in the States.

We left the court. In the hallway one of my brothers handed me a Brazilian passport bearing the name William Frederico Assali and the picture of a bundled three-week-old baby. I was amazed by how fast things could be done in Brazil if you were willing to spend money. Yet a chill went through my body when I saw that passport. Yes, I had a baby, but could I get him an American visa? Would I have to fight with the U.S. Immigration authorities? Would I have to burden my mother and brothers?

I decided to keep Billy in the nursery until the day we were to leave for Los Angeles. I thought he would be better off there than in my mother's home.

I then rushed to my brother's wedding. The civil ceremony took place that afternoon at the home of the bride's parents. It was an impressive and joyous affair. Still more so was the religious ceremony, which was held in a big cathedral decorated with flowers. In both ceremonies my brothers and I dressed formally—top hats and tails. My mother and sister wore long formal gowns and wide-brimmed hats. It was the first time I had seen my mother dressed this way; she was radiant with happiness.

The bride marched down the aisle and was received by my brother, with me at his side. It seemed to me that the religious ceremony took forever to finish. My mind was on that little creature in the nursery. Would I get the visa on Monday? Would that baby be allowed to enter the States?

Fortunately, Sunday night I attended a farewell party for my brother and his bride, who were leaving for a honeymoon in the States. I say "fortunate" because I was sure I could not sleep, in anticipation of Monday. I asked my brother and his bride not to mention anything to Pauline, because I still was not sure if I would be returning with the baby.

At the appointed hour on Monday, I took Billy's passport to the consul's secretary. She met me in the corridor and told me to wait behind the elevators. I waited for about thirty minutes; it seemed an eternity. Suddenly she reappeared, beaming. She handed me the passport, wished me good luck, and told me to leave Brazil as soon as possible. How did she get the visa? I do not know to this day.

I took the streetcar back to my mother's home, looking at the visa more than twenty times. Although the seal of the United States government was there along with someone's signature, I was still afraid. My three-year struggle with Immigration had left scars. What if that visa was not the right one? What if the Immigration officer in the United States discovered that it was obtained in a dubious manner?

When I reached my mother's home, I called the airline, which said there was a flight leaving for Miami the following day at 2:00 P.M. I made reservations for myself and my youngest brother, Nassery, who was coming with me, and my three-week-old baby. They promised to give me a seat by a table in the rear of the plane where I could put the baby.

Next, I went to the nursery to get Billy. The staff had prepared three gallons of baby formula. I took the formula and Billy to my mother's home. At that time no ready-made diapers were available in the stores in Brazil. With my sister's help, my mother cut several bedsheets into diapers. Dr. Pontes's wife gave me a baby basket, a God-sent gift, because it made the task of caring for Billy on the flight much easier.

The following day, I went to the airport carrying Billy in one arm and a bottle of formula in the other; my brother carried the rest. We boarded the plane, an old DC-4, which left on time. It made many stops to refuel and take on provisions. I placed Billy's basket on the table next to my seat and kept hold of it all day and night. Although the temperature in the cabin fluctuated wildly, Billy slept through it all and woke up only for his formula or to have his diaper changed.

After about twenty-four hours in the air, we reached Miami, and Immigration. I lined up with the other passengers, Billy in the basket in one hand, my passport in the other. I had decided not to show Billy's passport unless asked. The officer looked at my passport carefully, stamped it, and handed it back to me. I had barely made a motion to leave when he said, "Wait a minute. What do you have in that basket?"

"A baby," I said.

"Where are his documents?" he asked sternly.

"I'm sorry," I said, "I forgot to show them to you." I pulled Billy's passport from my pocket and handed it to him.

He looked it over judiciously. "Where is the mother or the name of the mother of this child?"

I said, "This child has two mothers. One I don't know anything about. The other doesn't know anything about this baby."

He smiled and said, "Well, this is the first time we've seen a father surprising his wife with a baby; usually it's the other way around." These few kind words broke the tension. For the first time in many days, I relaxed.

I proceeded to the Customs section. By then the news had spread that a man had brought a baby with him from Brazil without his wife's knowledge. All the women in Customs crowded around Billy. Some changed his diaper, others gave him his bottle. All cooed.

I had planned to get more baby food at the Miami airport, but the departure of the flight to Chicago was announced before I could do so. I grabbed Billy's basket and just barely reached the plane before the door closed; it was the same one we had come on from Brazil. Between Miami and Chicago I ran out of baby food and diapers. I solved the problem of diapers by using napkins the stewardesses gave me. But they had only one can of powdered milk left.

Billy began screaming for food just before we landed at O'Hare Airport, at 10:30 P.M. In 1957, O'Hare was still under construction, and a small cafeteria was the only source of food. Besides, we had to make a connection from Chicago's Midway Airport to Los Angeles at 12:30 A.M. Billy cried all the way from O'Hare to Midway, a bus ride that lasted more than one hour. At Midway I rushed to the cafeteria, where I quieted Billy with some milk diluted with tea. Then I found out, to my horror, that we had no reservations and that all flights to Los Angeles were fully booked. After frantic negotiating with several airlines, we finally got on the 1:30 flight. I called Pauline immediately, asked her to meet us, but said nothing about the baby.

As soon as the airplane took off, two stewardesses and several women passengers offered to take care of Billy. They saw that I was exhausted and on the verge of collapse; I had not slept in over twenty-eight hours. Feeling that he was in good hands, I leaned back and fell asleep in less than three minutes. I did not wake up until the airplane was over the Los Angeles airport. When the plane came to a final stop, someone shouted: "Let the man with the baby go first." The women were especially eager to see Pauline's reaction.

As I walked down the steps, I saw my newlywed brother and his bride, Robin, and Pauline waiting near the exit. When I reached Pauline, I opened the basket and said, "Meet Billy." She almost fainted.

As soon as we got home I called Dr. Arthur Parmelee, a pediatrician and good friend. He rushed over, examined Billy, and gave Pauline basic instructions on how to take care of a baby. We also called the Dignams and other friends with small children. They came over with diapers, bottles, and other essentials.

By noon that day the good news had spread in the neighborhood and among the UCLA faculty members. A stream of people bearing all kinds of gifts came to our home over the next two weeks. Many of our friends wanted to put the news in the paper, particularly the consul's request for the anti-Communist affidavit. Reporters from *Life* magazine asked me to give them the story and let them take pictures. I refused all requests and prohibited all publicity. Within the next two weeks the situation quieted down, and I went back to work.

24 · Animal Model for Pregnancy Research

GOOD news greeted me when I returned to work. Prior to leaving for Brazil, I had invited some excellent young obstetricians and gynecologists to join our department. I now learned that Donald Hutchinson, who had been trained with Albert Pleutl at Columbia University on placental transport in primates, had already been hired. John Kelly, another fine teacher and an investigator into the effects of pressure exerted on the fetal head during birth, was to join us shortly. Dr. Hans Simmer, of the Max Planck Institute in Germany, who had worked with the famous Professor A. Butenandt, had accepted our offer and was to join us within six months. He was an endocrinologist in both the clinical and investigative fields.

In 1957 the National Institutes of Health had initiated a new system of grants for training young postgraduates in research and for academic careers in all branches of medical sciences. Only departments with an excellent reputation and conclusive proof of research and academic capabilities could qualify. We had applied for a large training grant early in 1957. Six months later our application was approved and we were given the first training grant in obstetrics and gynecology in the country, which was considered a great honor. Lawrence Longo, who was to become one of the leading experts in placental physiology, became our first trainee.

When our team debated finding an animal species for our experimental model for pregnancy research, including experimental induction of toxemia, we considered two species: the sheep and the monkey. Each had its advantages and disadvantages.

The sheep had been and still is the traditional animal for research on the fetus and the newborn. It is a docile animal; experiments can be carried out under local, spinal, or general anesthesia. The fetus is relatively large (similar in weight to the human fetus), and its blood vessels are big enough to be suitable for various circulatory measurements, particularly blood flow. The gestation is sufficiently long to allow studies of the various maternal and fetal changes. The only disadvantage of the sheep, so we then thought, was that the placenta is structurally somewhat dissimilar to that of humans and could present slight problems in transferring information from the sheep's placental functions to those of the human. As it turned out, this small difference did not have much effect on the basic results.

On the other hand, the placental structures of primates (monkeys) resemble those of humans more than sheep's do. But the monkey is an excitable animal and difficult to work with except under general anesthesia—a type of anesthesia that usually alters many of the body's functions in both mother and fetus. Furthermore, the fetal monkey is relatively small and fragile and its vessels less suitable for measurements of circulatory functions than those of the sheep.

We decided to use both species and divide our research team between them. One group, headed by Hutchinson, was to work with monkeys and concentrate on placental functions and transfer. The other group, headed by me, would work with sheep, elucidating the cardiovascular functions as they adjust to intrauterine life before and after birth, and their controlling mechanisms. In this animal an attempt would also be made to reproduce toxemia of pregnancy as it occurs in humans. We thought the monkey would be more suitable for this project, but preliminary experiments showed that the blood pressure of the monkey changes considerably from one minute to another merely because of excitement. Stable blood pressure could be obtained in the monkey only under anesthesia, which alters the control. Furthermore, we had learned from veterinarians that pregnant sheep develop a disease similar in many respects to human toxemia of pregnancy. So we settled on the sheep for experimental toxemia, as well as for most of the research programs on adjustment to intrauterine life and changes after birth. This decision brought back to me memories of my boyhood in Rachaya and my life as a shepherd. To become involved with sheep again after more than thirty years and under totally different circumstances gave me much pleasure.

But sheep could not be housed in commercial cages and could not breed in the confined space available at UCLA; they required the open areas of a farm or a corral. UCLA was located in a heavily urban and highly expensive residential area, so breeding sheep within or around the campus was also out of the question. We tried schools in the San Fernando Valley, including Pierce College, which had facilities for sheep, goats, and horses. But after six months we gave this up, mainly because we could not control the mating time and we were not allowed to reproduce toxemia of pregnancy.

Finally a collaborative program was established between our group and a group at the School of Veterinary Medicine of the University of California at Davis, headed by Drs. Louis Holm and Harold Parker. A herd

of good-quality ewes was purchased and placed in a corral with four or five rams. The people at Davis could tell
when a ram mounted a female sheep and whether or not
it made her pregnant.

When pregnant sheep became available, I flew to Sac-
ramento every Monday morning for the 145 to 160 days
of the pregnancy. Holm or one of his associates would
pick me up at the airport and drive me to Davis, where
we would work ten to fourteen hours each day on experiments. I would go back to Los Angeles on Friday to
spend the weekend with my family and check on activities at UCLA.

To produce toxemia in the sheep, we had to impose
some form of stress on a special breed of animals that had
twins or triplets and that were close to term. After several trials, we decided that the easiest and most effective
way to do this was to drive them on a two-to-three-mile
walk in the rain. The rain would soak their wool and
make them heavy and tired, thus producing the stress
that can produce the disease. With the help of some of
the technicians, we performed this herding job whenever it rained. Sure enough, a number of the animals
developed sheep toxemia of pregnancy. We studied these
animals thoroughly. Although their disease had many
similarities to human toxemia, it had some differences as
well. Yet we learned a great deal and collected a vast
store of information that proved extremely helpful.

25 · Project Scandia

THE overall developmental work on the flowmeter, including the miniaturization of the probes and amplifying and recording systems, had progressed rapidly after
our first demonstration at the Los Angeles convention.
Subsequent improvements and modifications were
made, resulting in an instrument far superior to any
other for measuring the rate of blood flow.

Despite this progress, Tubovki, the biophysicist in
charge of that part of the project, began showing some
emotional and behavioral problems. He completely dis-
trusted everyone working in the laboratory and imag-
ined constantly that someone was stealing the "secrets"
of the flowmeter. I was the only one who escaped suspicion. After all, he depended on me, not only for money
and space to pursue the research, but also for promotion
and tenure.

Because of his suspicions, he requested that we change
all the locks in the laboratories every three months. His
desk was always locked and the drawers heavily bolted.
Every night he carried home in two bulging briefcases
every piece of paper related to the flowmeter, then
brought them back the following morning. I brushed all
this aside as irrelevant, because we were making significant progress in the flowmeter instrumentation. I was
convinced that, with patience, we would achieve a major

breakthrough. So I went along with the changing of locks, but resisted as much as possible his requests for replacing personnel, since this would destroy all continuity in the work. Obviously, every time we replaced a technician, the new one would have to be trained from scratch, which was time-consuming and delayed the project. Despite my efforts to stop them, some technicians left because they could not tolerate the atmosphere of suspicion in the lab.

Finally, toward the end of 1957, the flowmeter was developed to a point where we felt it could be tried on humans. We had already tried it on various animal species, pregnant and nonpregnant, and it had proved safe and efficient. To give the flowmeter a trial on pregnant humans in the United States was extremely difficult, if not impossible. The red tape that resulted from restrictions on human experimentation required months of work.

Sweden, Denmark, and Finland, on the other hand, had had legalized abortion laws for years, making those countries the mecca for research on small fetuses obtained through abortion. I got in touch with a team of investigators at the Karolinksa Institute, the main hospital and research center of Stockholm University, and also with a group at the University of Turku, in Finland. I proposed to them a collaborative research project on measuring the rate of blood flow to the pregnant uterus through the gestational age in which they performed abortions. In addition, I suggested that we attempt to measure the blood flow in the umbilical cord before the fetus is removed from the uterus, and at the same time analyze the oxygen content entering the uterus through the arteries and leaving through the veins. The same measurements would be made in the fetus.

By establishing the rate of blood flow and the difference in the quantity of oxygen entering and leaving the uterus, we would know the amount of oxygen consumed by the pregnant uterus or transferred to the fetus. Likewise, by making the same measurements in the fetus, we would know the quantity of oxygen consumed by the fetus per unit of tissue. This type of research was entirely new; the data we hoped to derive from it would provide basic and badly needed information on how the fetus lives inside the uterus, submerged in a bag of water and depending on the little oxygen that comes from its mother.

These ideas dated back to the English physiologist William Harvey. When Harvey first described the circulation of the blood in the early seventeenth century, he observed that the fetal blood was darker than the maternal blood. He had no way of knowing why, because the properties of oxygen in living organisms were as yet unknown. His observations were ignored for more than two centuries until, late in the nineteenth century, two German scientists stated for the first time that fetal blood was less oxygenated than maternal blood. This statement was not experimentally proved until 1927, when English investigators devised methods to collect blood samples from fetal vessels. Analysis of these samples invariably revealed oxygen levels considerably lower than adult blood levels.

These observations led to the time-honored concept that the fetus lives inside the uterus in a state of hypoxia or asphyxia. To dramatize this concept, the phrase "Mount Everest in Utero" was coined, comparing the fetus inside the uterus to a person living at the peak of Mount Everest. This concept, based on simple blood analyses, prevailed up to the time we started our work. Some obstetricians still believe it.

When we started working in this field, we had no

doubt whatsoever but that previous investigators were correct. Fetal blood was unquestionably less oxygenated than maternal. Maternal blood had an oxygen tension of about one hundred millimeters of mercury, while fetal blood had about twenty. Our reasoning went beyond mere qualitative analyses of blood-oxygen levels. We knew that the uptake of oxygen or of any other substance by the body or by any tissue does not depend only on the quantity of oxygen or of that substance present in a sample of blood; it depends also on the rate of blood flowing and delivering oxygen or any other substance to the tissue. This was the Fick principle, known to physiologists for many years.

What had prevented past investigators from applying the Fick principle to the fetus was their lack of means for measuring the rate of blood flow that brings oxygen from the mother to the fetal tissues. By the end of 1957, we felt we had evolved such a method, so our first task was to test the Mount Everest in Utero concept to see whether the fetus indeed lives in a state of hypoxia or asphyxia. The teams in Stockholm and Turku agreed to our proposal and welcomed the collaboration. They suggested we arrive in the early spring, to avoid the cold winter and the midsummer vacation period. The expedition was labeled "Project Scandia" and was fully supported by NIH.

With the help of some technicians, Tubovki and I packed the necessary equipment to be shipped by air freight to Stockholm. A few parts were not included because they had not yet arrived from the suppliers. In late March we flew to England, where some lectures had been scheduled for us at the University of London, and on to Edinburgh, Scotland, and more lectures.

We arrived at Stockholm and took rooms at the Palace Hotel, near the hospital. On the following day we met the members of the Swedish team and were shown the area near the delivery room where the equipment was to be installed. Although one of the Swedish scientists then accompanied us to a Customs warehouse to help in the release of our equipment, Tubovki was annoyed. He thought that the Swedes should already have released the equipment and had it installed. Obviously this was absurd, because the equipment was in our names, and our Swedish collaborators had no authorization to receive it. Furthermore, they knew nothing about the flowmeter and could not possibly have installed it. But logical arguments were of little avail.

At the hospital we opened the boxes and began sorting out and putting together the various parts of the instrumentation. It was then that Tubovki lost his self-control. Two things set him off: first, some cables, with their appropriate connections, were missing (I was under the impression that they were to arrive in a separate package later); and second, our instrumentation was made to operate on a 110-volt current, and the Swedish current was 220 volts. These two small setbacks plunged him into deep despair. He hurled accusations at the technicians in Los Angeles, calling them traitors who were trying to sabotage the expedition. He also leveled all kinds of charges at the Swedish scientists, but fortunately he did it in their absence. I tried everything to quiet him and dispel his gloom, but without success.

The chairman of the Pharmacology Department at Karolinska sent his engineer to help us solve our technical problems. The engineer, Allan Westersten, saved Project Scandia from complete and dismal failure and had the greatest impact on the development and improvement of the subsequent models of the flowmeter.

First he met with Tubovki and me for about two hours, during which we explained to him the theoretical and practical principles of the flowmeter, the various parts of the instrumentation, and the problems we were having in obtaining good flow signals. At the end of that meeting Westersten had not only grasped the entire spectrum of the technical aspects of the flowmeter, but also found the reasons for our difficulties and offered a solution. While he spoke, Tubovki's face clouded with suspicion.

That evening Tubovki came to my room and stated that he wanted to work things out by himself; if he found later that he needed Westersten, he would ask for him. I said, "Why did you suddenly change your mind? Westersten knows the problems, knows where to find parts, and can expedite the solution. We need to start working."

He was highly suspicious, as usual. "Westersten already knows too much about the flowmeter," he said. "He's a smart fellow. If we let him learn any more, he may give the secret of the flowmeter construction to some people in Sweden."

I was both disgusted and discouraged. I argued that his attitude was going to ruin the project. I pointed out that our clinical collaborators, who were to perform the operative procedure on the patients, were beginning to lose interest, and if we kept tinkering around, they might withdraw from the project entirely.

Tubovki proceeded to give me a full history of his family background, to which he attributed his emotional problems and suspicious nature. The conversation lasted until 2:00 A.M. Finally he said, "Give me two days to try to solve the problems by myself. If I don't, we'll have another talk." Before two days had elapsed, Tubovki came to see me. He was very disturbed. He said he believed he had been sabotaged and it was useless for him to keep working on the project.

Somehow I scraped together every ounce of patience and composure left me. I told him that I assumed all responsibilities for our problems and for not making the proper preparations. Then I said, "I believe it would be better for your health, and for all of us, if you withdrew from this project and returned to the States. You may want to take a little vacation in Europe before you go back."

He promptly accepted my suggestion and left Stockholm the following day. I felt a tremendous sense of relief; I was certain that we could now proceed smoothly. And that was exactly what happened.

Allan Westersten assumed technical command of the instrumentation and solved all the difficulties. In the next two or three days we collected data from the first patient, and in the remaining two weeks we studied five patients. Then Dr. John Lind, the chairman of the Pediatrics Department at Karolinska, advised us to move on to Turku, Finland, where, he said, there were more patients and fewer restrictions on human research. Lauri Rauramo, of the Obstetrics and Gynecology Department, alerted the Finnish team and arranged for a yacht to take the equipment to Turku. Twenty-four hours later we were installed in the delivery rooms of the Turku University Hospital, where we stayed for about two months.

Drs. L. Hervonen, C. Hartiala, and others at the university assisted in the blood-chemistry analyses and other experimental details. We collected a tremendous amount of information on human pregnancy of eight to twenty-four weeks, including data on blood flow and on oxygen consumption on both the maternal and fetal sides. In addition, Dr. B. Westin had developed an artificial womb containing liquid similar to the amniotic fluid and had devised a perfusion system to keep small fetuses alive while in this womb. We studied a number of fetuses in this artificial system and learned a great deal about the impact of temperature, oxygen, acidity, and other factors on the various body functions. All these experiments were recorded on color film, which was later shown at universities, medical meetings, and medical associations all over the world.

On the final day in Turku, we celebrated our success with a party such as only Scandinavians can give. I urged Allan Westersten to come to America and continue work on the flowmeter; he was single and had a love of adventure, so he promptly accepted my offer. One week after I returned to the States, he arrived. We made a good team and have continued our collaboration to this day.

After I came back from Europe I took a week's vacation and stayed home to play with Billy and celebrate his first birthday.

On my first day at work I had the surprise of my life. I found the laboratories all locked. They had never been locked before, because assistants and technicians were in and out all the time. I opened one door with my key and found a desolate and depressing sight. The labs had been stripped of all instrumentation and tools except for some screwdrivers, pliers, and a table used for animal surgery. All the expensive equipment bought with my grant money was gone. Even the technicians had been dismissed; the place was deserted. Although I had an idea who was responsible for this, I decided not to waste time on it any longer. With the help of Allan Westersten and other engineers and technicians, I reassembled a complete and efficient electronic and animal-research laboratory, in which a number of innovations were introduced in the methods of measuring blood flow, oxygen, and other elements in the blood of the mother and the fetus. These studies broke new ground in maternal-fetal medicine and contributed to the creation of a new discipline, called perinatology. They were later to earn me many awards.

26 · Mysteries
of Intrauterine Life

THE results of the experiments we conducted in the Scandinavian countries on small human fetuses provided us with startling information. First, we confirmed what we and others had shown in animal and human pregnancy, that the difference in blood oxygenation was large even in the smallest fetus studied; just as in term pregnancy, the mother had an oxygen tension of about one hundred millimeters of mercury, the fetus about twenty. The amazing thing was that these measurements were the same in women and sheep, at term or early in pregnancy. These findings ruled out the size and shape of the placenta as important factors in placental transfer. Second, we observed that the rate of blood flow that carries oxygen to fetal tissues was relatively high; when such flow was calculated on the basis of the fetal weight unit, it turned out to be four to five times greater than in the adult animal.

With these data in hand, we applied the Fick principle, multiplying the rate of flow by the differences in blood oxygen of the arterial and venous blood. The results of these calculations showed that the fetal tissues were receiving and consuming exactly the same quantity of oxygen per unit of weight as the adult organism, despite the fact that the level of oxygen in the fetal blood was considerably lower. The obvious conclusion derived from these observations was that, although the fetal blood looked hypoxic when judged by adult standards, the fetal tissues were not. The low oxygen level of the fetal blood was compensated for by a high rate of blood flow. Hence, under normal conditions the fetal tissues were just as well oxygenated as those of the adult.

Before publishing these results, we thought it essential to confirm our findings in other animal species, with which we had more freedom of experimentation and measurement. We expected that these results would have an enormous impact on the scientific community. So we outlined a series of experimental protocols to be carried out step by step over the next ten years, until we had explored fully the role of oxygen in fetal life before and after birth.

The first series of experiments was performed on fetal sheep, mature and premature. We repeated what we had done with the human fetus in the Scandinavian countries. In addition, we attempted to measure the volume of blood that the heart delivers to the fetal body per minute, which is known scientifically as the output of the heart. In the adult, such measurement is not too difficult to perform, because the right side of the heart ejects all its output into the pulmonary artery, which brings it to the lung to be oxygenated; from the lung, the blood returns to the left side of the heart, from which it is ejected into the aorta, which distributes the blood to the rest of the body. Hence, in the adult the output of the right side is the same as that of the left, and either is accessible to measurement.

In the fetus, on the other hand, there is a large blood vessel connecting the main pulmonary artery to the aorta, called the ductus arteriosus. This blood vessel, or shunt, diverts the largest amount of blood ejected by the right ventricle away from the lungs and directly into the aorta. The main reason for this diversion is that in the fetus the lungs do not function as respiratory organs to oxygenate the blood; the fetal blood is oxygenated in the placenta. The presence of the ductus arteriosus, along with an opening between the two heart chambers, makes the technique of measuring the output of the fetal heart extremely difficult and renders the methods used on the adult inapplicable. The difficulties are compounded by the fact that the ductus is closed after birth, by mechanisms discovered only recently.

Because of the anatomical complexity of the fetal heart and its blood vessels, we had to devise a new method to measure the fetal cardiac output. This method consisted of placing one flowmeter around the ductus arteriosus and another around the aorta where it emerges from the left ventricle. Since the blood flow of these two vessels is distributed to the whole body, the sum constitutes the fetal cardiac output. Allan Westersten and his co-workers in our laboratory had devised a new flowmeter model, entirely different from and considerably more accurate than the one constructed before. In a short time they completed two units for us with which we began measuring the rate of blood flow in the ductus arteriosus and ascending aorta in fetal lambs. All our measurements showed that the output of the heart in the fetus was three to four times greater per unit of weight than that of the adult. These measurements provided additional confirmation of our previous conclusions that the low level of blood oxygen in the fetus is compensated for by a high rate of blood flow not only in the umbilical cord but also through the heart output.

Other series of experiments carried out on pregnant rats, guinea pigs, and rabbits provided the final incontrovertible proof of our theory. An investigator named George Misrahy had been working at the Children's

Hospital in Los Angeles on a new polarographic method of measuring tissue oxygen. The method consisted of implanting thin, specially made wires in various tissues of the body. These wires were connected to specialized equipment by which relative values of tissue oxygen level could be monitored. We persuaded Misrahy to join our team. Together we began monitoring simultaneously the tissue oxygen level in the brain, kidney, and muscle of mother and fetus of rats, rabbits, and guinea pigs. The results showed clearly that the levels of oxygen in the tissues of both mother and fetus were the same, despite the fact that their blood oxygen was markedly different.

Having obtained much confirmation, we finally published our results, proving conclusively that the fetus does not live inside the uterus in a hypoxic or asphyxic condition, and therefore that the concept of Mount Everest in Utero was a myth.

Our experiments of measuring the blood flow in the ductus arteriosus and the aorta of the fetal lamb revealed the magnitude of fetal cardiac output and its importance in oxygenating fetal tissues. But these same experiments left another question unanswered: Why does the oxygen level in fetal blood have to be that low? There had to be a reason. To find it, we decided to perform two series of experiments on pregnant sheep. In the first series we would raise the oxygen level of the mother's blood from one hundred to five hundred millimeters of mercury while observing the effects on the fetal level of oxygen and the blood flow through its blood vessels; this series was labeled the "hyperoxia" experiments. In the second series we would lower the oxygen level of the mother by making the ewe breathe a gas mixture poor in oxygen; again, we would observe the effects on the fetus. These were the "hypoxia" experiments.

These experiments provided perplexing results, to say the least. The hyperoxia experiments showed that increasing the maternal blood oxygen level fivefold increased fetal blood oxygen by only about fifteen to twenty percent. It seemed, then, that there were limiting factors or barriers that kept the blood level of oxygen in the fetus low. Yet these factors did not seem to operate after birth, since when the fetus was born and took its first breath, the oxygen level in its blood rose markedly. On the other hand, the hypoxia experiments showed two things: that it was necessary to lower the maternal oxygen levels considerably in order to decrease the fetal oxygen somewhat, and that the fetus could tolerate a great deal of oxygen curtailment, even an amount that would kill an adult in less than two minutes.

At the same time that we were trying to influence fetal oxygenation by raising or lowering maternal oxygen levels, we were also recording blood flow, blood pressure, vascular resistance, and heart rate on both the maternal and the fetal side. The monitoring of fetal circulation suggested some relation between the level of fetal blood oxygen and the way the fetal circulation functions: it appeared that the low oxygen level in the fetal blood was purposely designed by whoever created this world. Nagging questions remained: How does oxygen influence fetal circulation? What particular vascular structures in the fetus are under the influence and control of oxygen?

The simplest way to answer these questions was to raise the oxygen level in the fetal blood without having to inflate and ventilate the fetal lungs. This had to be done through oxygenating the mother to extremely high levels, because the ordinary means of doing this failed to produce a level of fetal blood oxygen similar to that which occurs after birth, since the placental or biochemical barrier prevented the fetus from raising its oxygen levels proportionally to the mother's. But before we could devise a method to do this we decided to monitor the various circulatory functions of the fetus while it was still in the uterus with its blood oxygen at the fetal level; the monitoring was to continue without interruption when the fetus was delivered and took its first breath and when its lungs were expanded with air or oxygen. In these experiments we were recording simultaneously the pressures in the four chambers of the heart as well as in the pulmonary artery and aorta. We were also recording the blood flow in the aorta, the ductus arteriosus, and the main pulmonary artery. Obviously this difficult research required a well-organized team, which fortunately we had.

The first experiment of this extraordinary project was carried out on a day that will long remain imprinted on the minds of Americans: November 22, 1963. We started the experiments rather early that day, knowing it would be a long and difficult research procedure. By 10:00 A.M. all the catheters, flowmeters, and other instrumentation to monitor the various circulatory parameters and blood gases from mother and fetus were in place and functioning perfectly. We could read the pressure of each of the four chambers of the fetal heart and of its two major vessels, as well as the blood flows of all the great vessels, which were being recorded simultaneously for the first time in history.

In our laboratory it had been, and still is, the custom, whenever a major experiment was under way, to turn off the radio and answer only emergency phone calls. Hardly had we started to make the first part of the recording when a technician and a secretary burst into the laboratories, shouting, "President Kennedy has been shot!" Everyone in the laboratory was stunned.

"Let's terminate the experiment and close everything

for the day," I said. But Dr. John Morris, who was a trainee in our program, sent by the U.S. Army, felt that our experiment was too important for mankind and for science to be halted. "Although I'm deeply grieved by this tragedy," he said, "I don't want to see the experiment stopped." Dr. Ronald Smith, the other trainee, seconded Morris's sentiment, as did technicians and engineers. I was overruled. I told them to proceed with the experiment and I went to another room to be alone for a while.

I had several reasons to feel the loss of John F. Kennedy more keenly than my co-workers. Aside from my loyalty to the liberal faction of the Democratic party, I had a deep affection for Kennedy personally and great hopes for his social and political programs.

Shortly after he became President his wife had lost a premature baby, and several of us in maternal-fetal-neonatal research petitioned him to create a special institute within the National Institutes of Health to support research and health care in this field. Within a short period of time Kennedy created the National Institute of Child Health and Human Development, which became a great stimulus for research in the area of reproduction.

The series of experiments that began on the day of President Kennedy's assassination lasted for over three years. Subsequently, several phases of the research were repeated in various animal species at different periods of gestation and after birth. When all the pieces of the puzzle were put together they showed startling results:

One: When the fetus is still in the uterus, its lungs filled with fluid, the resistance in the blood vessels that feed the lungs is very high. Consequently, the pressure in the lung vessels is very high (eight to ten times that of the adult) and the rate of blood flow in the lungs is very low; most of the blood that is supposed to go to the lungs, as in the neonate or adult, is shunted away through the ductus arteriosus. Also, because of the high pressure in the lung vessels, the pressure in the right side of the heart (the part of the pump that ejects the blood to the lungs) is equally high, considerably more so than in the adult.

Two: The resistance and pressure in the vascular network that supplies blood to the rest of the fetal body, including the placenta, are relatively low, certainly lower than in the lung vessels. This pressure gradient favors shunting the blood from the right side away from the lungs toward the aorta. The umbilical-placental circulation is mainly responsible for low resistance and low pressure in the aorta and its branches.

Three: When the infant is born and takes its first breath spontaneously, or its lungs are ventilated artificially, the oxygen level in the fetal blood rises from about twenty to fifty millimeters of mercury or more; the pressure and resistance in the lung blood vessels fall precipitously; the ductus arteriosus that was shunting blood starts to close, and almost all the blood ejected by the right ventricle now goes to the lungs to be oxygenated. The placenta ceases to be the main route of oxygen to the fetus.

Four: When the umbilical cord connecting the fetus to its mother through the placenta is cut, the pressure in the aorta and its branches rises and becomes higher than that in the lungs—a situation opposite to that of the fetus.

In summary, then, the salient transitional changes that occur in the fetus immediately after birth are the expansion of the lung alveoli, with the elimination of fluid and the oxygenation of the blood, followed by a marked increase in lung blood flow and closure of the ductus arteriosus.

These conclusive observations provided clarification of many aspects of fetal life in utero, but also raised important questions, the answers to which were needed to settle the problems of oxygen and its role in the fetus. The first question was: Would the rise in blood oxygen that occurs after birth be the factor responsible for opening up the lung vessels and closing the ductus arteriosus? And, as a corollary: Would the low oxygen level that prevails in fetal blood serve to keep the ductus open and the blood vessels of the lungs constricted, so that most of the blood not needed by the lungs is shunted away?

The existing literature on this subject had a slight hint about the effect of oxygen on the ductus. Joseph Barcroft and his associates in England had observed some narrowing of the ductus when the lungs of fetal guinea pigs were inflated, but these experiments were very crude and inconclusive. Most of the literature attributed the opening of the blood vessels in the lung, with the attendant fall in pressure and increase in blood flow, to a mere physical phenomenon related to expanding the lung alveoli with air, instead of their being filled with fluid as in the fetus. In fact, there were abundant experimental data showing that expansion of the fetal lungs with nitrogen, an inert gas, produced the same immediate effects as oxygen. Therefore, though our series of experiments pointed strongly toward an oxygen role, they did not rule out the mechanical expansion of the lungs with air as a cause.

There was only one way to resolve this dilemma—a way that we had tried once without success. The decisive proof of the relation of oxygen to the lung blood vessels and the ductus would be to oxygenate the fetal blood to the level reached in the neonate but without allowing the fetus to breathe or to expand its lung alveoli. We had already attempted to do this by giving the mother one hundred percent oxygen to breathe, but because of certain complex anatomical and biochemical circumstances, this amount of oxygen was insufficient to raise the fetal oxygen to neonatal levels.

One last resort remained open to us, though it presented some risk to the investigators. This involved putting the pregnant ewe with her fetus still in her uterus in a hyperbaric oxygen chamber. Both the mother and the fetus would be instrumented as in the other series of experiments. After recording all blood oxygen levels and circulatory measurements with the chamber at sea level (normal fetal state), we would then elevate the pressure in the chamber to three atmospheres. Our mathematical calculations showed that this should raise the maternal oxygen level to 3,000 millimeters of mercury, a level that should then overcome whatever barriers existed and should raise fetal blood oxygen to very high levels without expanding the lungs.

There was only one hyperbaric oxygen chamber in the Los Angeles area, and it was used for the treatment of humans. It was at the Good Samaritan Hospital, about twenty miles east of UCLA. After some persuasive negotiations we were given permission to use it for animal experiments. We moved all our recording instrumentations and surgical equipment, then began taking pregnant sheep to Good Samaritan in a truck.

Mother and fetus were operated on and instruments placed in their respective vessels inside the chamber. First we recorded all the measurements at normal oxygen level, including blood flow and pressure in the fetal lung and blood flow in the ductus and ascending aorta. Then we closed the chamber and increased its inside pressure to three atmospheres, with additional oxygen given to the ewe through a nasal tube.

The results were most thrilling to us and were scientifically convincing. In every case we observed that as the fetal oxygen level began to surpass fifty millimeters of mercury, the ductus arteriosus closed and the lung blood vessels opened. In other words, we were transforming a fetus still in the uterus into a neonate merely by elevating its blood oxygen level. Then, when the chamber pressure was lowered again to one atmosphere (sea level), the fetal blood oxygen returned to its low level, the ductus reopened, and the lung blood vessels constricted again.

When the series of hyperbaric oxygen experiments was completed and all the records and data were analyzed, a clear and precise picture emerged of the role of oxygen in fetal and neonatal states. The information left no doubt that the low oxygen level is specifically "designed" by nature, God, or whomever for the fetal circulation to function as such during intrauterine life. Such a low oxygen level serves to keep the vessels of the lungs constricted, so that little blood circulates through them—a logical design, since the lungs do not act as oxygenating organs during that period of development. At the same time the low oxygen tension maintains the ductus arteriosus wide open, so that as much blood as possible can be shunted away from the lungs toward the aorta and the rest of the body.

The presence of this wide shunt, the ductus, serves in turn to provide the fetus with a high cardiac output and a high rate of umbilical-placental blood flow, to compensate for the low oxygenation of the fetal blood. In this way, and taking into consideration the weight unit, the fetal tissues can have the same oxygen uptake as those of an adult. After birth, and with the first breath, this cheap element oxygen—which exists in the air, and for which no mother or father has to pay—enters the lungs and within minutes transforms fetal circulation into neonatal circulation. When the oxygen level reaches forty to fifty millimeters of mercury, the ductus arteriosus begins to close and the pulmonary vessels to open. Interruption of the umbilical cord aids this process by raising the pressure in the aorta, thereby aiding in the cessation of flow through the ductus.

One more task remained in our study of oxygen's role in fetal circulation. We had to find out whether oxygen was acting on the ductus directly or through the nervous system. To answer this question, we removed ductus vessels from fetal lambs and perfused them by an artificial system outside the body in media in which the oxygen level was lowered or raised. We found out that oxygen acts directly on the vessel walls. Later studies by other investigators showed that these vessels have oxygen receptors which are sensitive to changes in levels of blood oxygen.

At long last we had in hand the various processes that operate through birth and in the immediate neonatal period to produce a healthy, normal baby. When one or more of these processes malfunctions, the blue baby syndrome results.

For instance, a premature baby with insufficiently inflated lungs, or with lungs coated with hyaline membranes, is unable to oxygenate its blood sufficiently. Consequently, the vessels in the lungs remain constricted, the pressure remains high, and the blood flow remains low. Under these circumstances the ductus arteriosus remains open, shunting poorly oxygenated blood to the aorta. The aorta distributes this somewhat dark blood to the infant's body. That infant looks blue because of the poorly oxygenated blood.

Also, a baby born either at term or prematurely may congenitally lack the oxygen receptors in the ductus arteriosus, or its pulmonary blood vessels may be unresponsive to oxygen because of congenital or anatomical abnormalities. These vessels will not allow enough blood to pass through the lungs to be oxygenated. Consequently, the various shunts present during fetal life remain open, thereby bringing poorly oxygenated blood to the infant's body. This infant, too, would be a blue baby.

A transitory blue baby syndrome may also result when a mother receives deep general anesthesia during delivery. The anesthesia agents pass into the fetus and depress its respiratory centers. With the clamping of the umbilical cord after birth, the anesthetic agent remains in the body, since the placenta is no longer available to eliminate it. The baby cannot expand its lungs sufficiently because of the depression of its respiratory centers. Under these circumstances the pressure in the pulmonary vessels remains high and the blood flow through the lungs low; the ductus arteriosus remains open, thereby shunting poorly oxygenated blood to the baby's body. This baby looks blue at birth, but may improve with prompt and appropriate treatment. If not adequately treated, however, the baby may continue to have a certain degree of pulmonary hypertension and a partially open ductus arteriosus, and may remain a blue baby for quite some time.

These same studies shed light not only on the multifaceted blue baby syndrome, but also on the mechanisms by which the fetus tolerates a high degree of maternal stress and more oxygen deprivation than the adult. It turns out that this tolerance results from the interplay of pulmonary circulation and the blood flow through the ductus arteriosus. Suppose, for instance, that a pregnant mother suffers an accident that causes loss of blood and throws her into circulatory shock. The blood flow through the pregnant uterus and placenta falls considerably during the state of shock, and this fall leads to a decline in the amount of oxygen transported to the unborn baby. The fall of the oxygen level in the blood of the fetus is sensed by the ductus arteriosus, which begins to dilate, while at the same time the blood vessels in the lungs begin to constrict. This double action makes it imperative that more blood be diverted from the lungs toward the fetal body through the ductus arteriosus. Hence the output of the fetal heart is elevated, which not only compensates for the low fetal oxygenation, but also maintains the perfusing pressure in the fetal circulatory system within normal range. Only when the oxygen deprivation is prolonged, and the compensatory mechanisms of the fetus begin to fall, does the fetus begin to show signs of distress that may end in its death.

The results of all these research projects, which started in 1958 and continued over a ten-year period, appeared in a long series of scientific reports published in medical journals. These reports generated a great deal of excitement among the scientific community, because they provided a rationale and scientific interpretation of many aspects of fetal life in utero and of the changes that occur after birth. They served as the basis for conferring on me the Virginia Apgar Award by the American Academy of Pediatrics.

By the late 1960s the research explosion in the field of reproduction, and particularly in the area related to the pregnant mother, the fetus, and the newborn, had produced such voluminous information as to warrant the publication of a book. At the beginning of 1967 I outlined, and then edited, a multiauthored two-volume treatise, entitled *Biology of Gestation.* The first volume, *The Maternal Organism,* covered biological changes, the formation of the ovum in the ovary, its fertilization by the sperm, the formation of the embryo, its transformation into a fetus, and the maternal organism's adjustment to pregnancy. The second volume, entitled *The Fetus and*

Neonate, covered the physiological and biochemical aspects of the fetus throughout its intrauterine life and the changes that occur after birth and throughout the early neonatal period. These two volumes were devoted to the normal behavior of the maternal, fetal, and neonatal organisms. A galaxy of prominent scientists from the United States and abroad contributed chapters, each reporting his own research while reviewing the relevant world literature.

Biology of Gestation appeared in 1968 and received extremely favorable reviews in medical journals all over the world. It was followed, in 1972 and 1973, by a three-volume work entitled *Pathophysiology of Gestation,* which at that time represented an innovative approach in medical writing. Developed out of our basic research, it explained how a normal function in the organism of the pregnant mother, the fetus, or the newborn could be altered to induce a given disease. The volumes were *Maternal Disorders, Fetal-Placental Disorders,* and *Fetal and Neonatal Disorders.*

27 · Death
of a Matriarch

IN Brazil during these years my family had made significant economic and social progress. In business, in addition to expanding the original store, they had opened several new retail branches, as well as their own factory to manufacture clothing. Some of them had gone into real estate and had made substantial fortunes. Each of my brothers, as well as my sister, had gotten married and now lived in their own homes, although all of them resided in the vicinity of the original house, still occupied by my mother. She continued to be the family's domineering and catalytic force. The rules dictated by the "Boss," my mother, required all of my brothers to meet with her at least three times a week for dinner. Also, the big lunch on Sunday was always in her home. Another rule was that whenever my brothers had any differences between themselves, whether related to business or to other problems, they were to go to her for arbitration. These rules were followed religiously until her death.

Socially my mother had gradually become the matriarch of the Syrio-Lebanese colony in São Paulo, particularly of those elements originating in Rachaya. She loved to entertain, to tell stories, to meet people and help them. She learned a few words of Portuguese, enough to get by in a grocery store. Arabic remained her main language, though she never learned to read or write it.

Her virtues were common sense, determination, frankness, and a fascinating personality. She could not imagine spending an evening alone; she was always with a large group, whether in her own home or at the homes of friends.

By 1950 my mother had developed a mild case of diabetes and a slight rise in blood pressure, and I asked one of my colleagues in São Paulo to look after her. The treatment of diabetes requires the patient's co-operation, particularly regarding diet. My mother was famous for cooking rich Arabic dishes and desserts heavy with sugar and butter, and she was also famous for eating them. The doctor told her that, in addition to taking regular shots of insulin, she had to go on a strict diet to lose at least thirty pounds. His advice fell on deaf ears. "I have lived my life. I enjoy everything I do or eat," was her response. "I'm not going to change because of diabetes!"

My colleague wrote me several times about his problems with my mother. He asked several former classmates of mine for support; he pleaded with my brothers and with friends of hers to persuade her to follow a diet. But it was all to no avail. She would take her insulin shots and eat rich food. On my visits to Brazil in 1953, 1957, and 1963, I tried everything in my power to prevail on her to follow the doctor's orders, but without success. In 1967 I was invited by a Latin American society for research on pregnant women to be the guest speaker during their annual meeting in Bahia, in the north of Brazil. After the meeting I flew to São Paulo to spend a few days with my family. For the first time in all those years, my mother was not the first one to greet me at the airport. My brothers said she was not feeling well. When I saw her, I was appalled by her physical condition. She had suffered a mild cerebral thrombosis that had paralyzed the left side of her face. In addition, she could not move as easily as before and would lie down to sleep after dinner. Yet her mental attitude, her biting sarcasm, and her love of people had not changed at all.

I stayed with her for a week. When the time came for me to leave, Uncle George and his wife, Alfredo's mother, helped my mother into the car, and the three took me to the airport. It was the last time I saw any of them alive.

In September of that year my mother suffered another mild stroke, from which she made a partial recovery. But in October the toes on both her feet turned blue, slowly became gangrenous, and fell off. She was by then totally bedridden and suffering incredible pain from the gangrene, which progressed inexorably up above her ankles.

My brothers called in the best doctors in town, among them one of my former professors of surgery, Alipio Correa. They were in unanimous agreement that my mother's legs had to be amputated above the knees. My brothers felt that I should make the final decision, and they telephoned me.

I had to think fast. I could not imagine my mother bedridden and without legs. I asked Correa, "How long will she live if we don't do anything but relieve the pain?"

"Less than six months" was the answer.

After an agonizing minute or so, I said, "Let her die with her legs. Please order any painkiller you can think of."

And that was that. My mother died two months later. I was not able to attend the funeral, because I was flat on my back with a herniated disc. But the Syrio-Lebanese colony in São Paulo paid her an affectionate last tribute. Six months later, Uncle George's wife died of a respiratory disease, and one year later Uncle George died of bladder cancer.

28 · The Battle for Medicare

ALTHOUGH I have never practiced medicine as a private physician, my association with the university hospitals at Cincinnati and at UCLA made me aware of the economic impact of medical costs, which had been rising year after year in the private office as well as in the hospital.

Although most of my time at UCLA was consumed by research and teaching, my national reputation as an expert in the management of obstetrical complications brought me in contact with complex and costly hospital cases. One in particular remains vivid in my mind, and it was probably the stimulus for my plunge some years later into the battle for a health-care bill for the aged.

Sometime in 1956, I was called by an obstetrician to see a severe case of convulsive toxemia at Hollywood Presbyterian Hospital. The patient was a young woman, the wife of a high-school teacher, and, like her husband, a Christian Scientist. She was in her thirtieth week of pregnancy and had received no prenatal care except monthly visits to her home by a Christian Scientist healer. She had developed all the signs and symptoms of severe toxemia, but it was not until she lost consciousness and had convulsions that the healer and her husband called a doctor.

When I saw her, I immediately realized that I was

faced with one of the most severe cases of convulsive toxemia I had ever seen. She was passing no urine at all, and her blood pressure was so high that it could not be read on the ordinary hospital instrument. She was moribund, and I did not think she would live twenty-four hours.

I started working on her in a desperate fight against death. I stayed with her in the hospital from eighteen to twenty hours a day, often sleeping there, so as to be close by if any crisis developed. She remained in a coma for twenty-seven days and had kidney shutdown for twenty-two. Extensive laboratory tests and other forms of diagnosis and treatment were performed. After the twenty-eighth day she become conscious and her kidneys started functioning. She expelled a dead fetus. Her blood pressure dropped to normal levels. Thirty-five days after admission, she was discharged, completely recovered.

Her hospital bills amounted to over $15,000, which at that time was an enormous sum. To pay the bills, her husband had to obtain a second mortgage on their house and sell his car and other valuables. He came and told me about this, then asked me for my bill. I told him to forget it.

This case, and many others, convinced me that continually rising medical costs were an enormous burden on the American people.

Prior to coming to the States, I was familiar with the activities of the American Medical Association and had a high regard for their accomplishments in establishing hospital standards and bringing about other improvements. I was not, however, aware at all of their political and socioeconomic stands on the major issues that faced medicine, its teaching, and its practice in hospitals and private offices.

Shortly after I began working at Cincinnati General

Hospital and became a member of the University of Cincinnati, I joined the local medical society. Oddly enough, at that time in Cincinnati there was no "closed-shop system" in organized medicine; I was able to join the Cincinnati society even though I was not a member of the state society and the AMA. I was too busy then with countless academic and nonacademic problems to worry about the views of organized medicine. I knew that President Truman had earlier proposed a system of federally supported health care, but I had no time to grasp its meaning or background.

Then in December 1949, after our research work on toxemia of pregnancy and its management had become well-known, I was invited by the AMA to address their clinical meeting in Denver, Colorado. After my talk on "Pathogenesis and Management of Toxemia," I wandered around the building and quite by accident ended up in a large ballroom where the AMA delegates were gathered for the business meeting. Eager to learn something about the organization, I decided to listen to the debates.

The delegates were discussing the federal government's proposal for a health bill. For several hours delegate after delegate denounced any government interference in the private practice of medicine. I heard suggestions on appropriating large sums of money to oppose, by any means available, anything that interfered with the prevailing system of private practice. Not a single voice was heard proposing any alternative, or advancing any new idea about helping patients who cannot pay medical and hospital expenses.

I took the plane back to Cincinnati somewhat disillusioned with the AMA. The hierarchy appeared to be composed of practicing physicians whose main concern was to preserve the private practice of medicine. Evidently they believed that they alone were qualified to pass judgment on the standards of medical care and its cost in the United States. Later I learned that they had opposed Blue Cross and other organizations that attempted to change the status quo.

When I joined the UCLA faculty, I was immediately asked to join the Los Angeles County Medical Society. Without the membership I could not work at a county hospital such as Harbor General. In my application I stated that I wanted membership in the Los Angeles County society only, emphasizing that I had no desire to join the state medical society or the American Medical Association. After a month I received a letter from the secretary of the Los Angeles County Medical Society stating unequivocally that I could not belong to the county society unless I also became a member of the state society and the AMA. The three memberships went together; none of the organizations gave separate memberships.

It was the most glaring example of a closed shop that I had ever seen. And it occurred at a time when many people in the United States, particularly members of the medical profession, were vehemently opposing the closed-shop system in industry and business. In fact, the AMA's system was worse than that of industry, because a doctor could not even get malpractice insurance unless he was a member of the local, state, and national organizations.

Although I felt greatly irritated at having to swear allegiance to the AMA before I could join the local medical organization, I had no choice but to accept their rules and pay the exorbitant three-in-one membership dues. I did not, however, attend a single meeting throughout the eight years of my membership, nor did I take any part in the activities of these organizations.

I was prompted to action during the presidential election campaign of 1960, when one of the major issues was health care for the elderly. Through its political arm, and with the help of state, county, and other groups of organized medicine, the AMA mobilized all its financial power to oppose any candidate who favored government assistance in health care. Each member was assessed extra dues, and millions of dollars were collected and allocated to fight any health-care bill suggested by the federal or state government.

During his campaign John Kennedy had promised that federal aid for health care for the aged would be among his top priorities. In the second year of his term, he proposed to Congress a health-care bill for people over sixty-five.

The AMA and its affiliate organizations immediately mobilized all their economic and political forces in every important city of the United States. Members campaigned in clubs and churches, in small and large communities, and even from door to door, against the health-care bill and exalted the virtues of private practice. Nowhere was the lobbying more lavish than in Washington, where the AMA had a battery of prominent and influential people working around the clock. They imported dissatisfied doctors from England and the Scandinavian countries to speak to the news media and testify before congressional committees against the evils of socialized medicine as practiced in those countries.

Shortly after Kennedy proposed the health-care bill, I resolved to campaign in its favor. I was convinced that medical care must not be allowed to continue escalating in cost, and that many people already could not afford it. Furthermore, in Cincinnati and other places I had seen the results of placing a price tag on medical practice.

Before I could act, I had to get around the university

regulations prohibiting faculty members from taking part in political activities using university affiliation. I approached Dan Morton, the chairman of our department, and told him I intended to campaign in favor of the Kennedy bill as a private citizen. I assured him that at no time would I make use of my position at the university or speak in the school's name. He replied that I could not take a political step such as this and remain a member of the county and state medical societies and of the AMA. I told him that I had long intended to resign anyway, because my philosophy did not agree with that of organized medicine. Moreover, malpractice insurance was handled for all of us by the regents, and I was engaged in animal research.

Morton stated gently that although he disagreed with me, he could not prevent me from taking any position I wished as an individual. He advised me, however, to clear the matter with the dean of the Medical School. I went to see Stafford Warren, who tried to persuade me to change my mind. My public opposition to organized medicine would antagonize my colleagues, he said, and make enemies. My answer was that a man has to live with his own conscience. The dean finally said that I must be sure not to involve the university in any speeches I made. I suddenly felt elated: the way now seemed clear for me to fight for the health-care bill.

My first step was to organize some support within the medical profession. Dr. Daniel Mishell, Sr., and a few others helped me draw up a list of forty or fifty doctors who were in favor of Kennedy's bill, and we set up a group called "Doctors' Organization in Favor of Health Care for the Aged." I was selected as its spokesman. Mrs. Mishell, who was active in Democratic party organizations, arranged a series of club and church meetings, where I lectured on the issue of medical care or debated it with representatives of organized medicine. I defended federal aid vehemently, using statistics compiled by the Department of Health, Education and Welfare to show how expensive medical care had become, and how many people were not treated because they could not afford to pay.

One day in 1961 CBS called to ask if I would debate the issue with representatives of organized medicine on prime-time television. The debate had been well advertised, and the network expected a good audience. Two representatives of organized medicine were to participate, but only one appeared. Each of us had ten minutes to present his case. My opponent spoke first and gave the usual argument: we already had the best medical care in the world; every patient had a choice of doctors. It was like hearing the same recording for the hundredth time. Then I presented data on our fetal and neonatal mortality, compared with nations where health care is governmentally supported, and quoted statistics on the cost of medical care and the burden it imposed on family finances. I spoke with feeling about the poor and neglected elderly who lived on Social Security and had to seek charity hospitals when they became ill. Then the moderator asked us both questions. I answered mine with facts and data; my opponent's answers were generalities on his earlier theme: we have the best care in the world. The minute the interview was over, my opponent left; I stayed and received congratulations from everyone in the studio, including the cameramen, the directors and producers, and several members of the audience.

The following day Morton and Warren congratulated me, even though they did not altogether agree with my position. Several other members of our faculty were most critical of the position I had taken and particularly of my having debated it on television. They said I was antagonizing the practicing physicians in the community, many of whom referred patients to UCLA.

One of them, an important department chairman, one of the founders of the medical school, and a friend of mine, went beyond a mere expression of disagreement. Two or three days after the debate, I was in line in the hospital cafeteria. I spotted him at the other end and greeted him. "Don't talk to me!" he barked. "You were disgraceful during the television debate in your opposition to the AMA." His anger mounting, he continued: "For twelve years I've been cultivating the goodwill of the community physicians, and in one stroke you destroy everything. What do you know about our system? You're a foreigner and you should keep your mouth shut!"

I was flabbergasted. "Don't you think we should discuss this privately in your office or mine?" I said in disbelief.

"No," he answered, and continued spouting insults at me.

Finally, I could take it no longer. "If you want to solve this argument your way, let's go outside and fight like animals!" I put my tray down on the table and stalked out of the cafeteria.

He did not speak to me again for some time, and he and nearly all of his staff were no longer socially friendly. Some years later, when I had pneumonia, I was admitted to UCLA Hospital. The day after my admission, the chairman entered my room and apologized for his behavior. This was, of course, long after Medicare had been passed and had proved lucrative for the medical profession.

Though the Kennedy health-care bill for the aged had been defeated in Congress, I was convinced that organized medicine had won a skirmish but would lose the war. Sure enough, Lyndon Johnson eventually made the health-care bill the law of the land, and the medical profession hailed it as a great thing. Indeed, it made many of them very rich very soon.

29 · Dan Morton's Retirement

BY the mid-sixties, the Department of Obstetrics and Gynecology at UCLA Medical Center had become one of the most prestigious and productive in the country, despite its relative youth. In original research in the field of maternal-fetal medicine, it was considered the leader in the United States, if not the world. Older and well-established universities sought people from UCLA and offered them positions in the Ob/Gyn departments at their universities. Jerry Moore became chairman at Columbia, Ted Quilligan at Yale, Don Hutchinson at the University of Pittsburgh; Luigi Mastrioni and John Kelly went to the University of Pennsylvania. This "sprinkling" of talent to other universities by a young institution led Nick Eastman, of Johns Hopkins, to acclaim, "Never in the history of medical education has such a young department produced so much talent in such a short period of time."

The man who was to a large extent responsible for this dynamic growth was the UCLA department chairman, Dan Morton. His liberal and kind attitude toward his associates served as an attraction to talented young specialists.

The agreement he and I had reached in Cincinnati—

namely, that he would be in charge of teaching and patient care and I in charge of research—was the cornerstone of our success. No other department in the country had such a well-defined division of responsibilities and such an integrated program of teaching and research. Dan gave me full authority and backing to expand the department and recruit the best young talent available. These new people were given faculty positions, each had teaching and clinical responsibilities, each became involved in research activities and published important papers in scientific journals. These men were consequently in great demand by other universities. By the mid-sixties, our department had become known as the "chairman's factory."

In 1965, Dan Morton announced that he would retire when he reached the age of sixty-five at the end of the 1966 academic year. I decided that this gentleman and superb human being should be given a retirement ceremony befitting him. I invited all his former and present residents, as well as all full-time and clinical Ob/Gyn faculty members, from both his days at the University of California, San Francisco, and his time at UCLA. I suggested that if they were unable to come, they send a letter or telegram that could be read aloud.

The ceremony was held in the Grand Ballroom of the Beverly Hilton Hotel. The dean, Dr. Sherman Mellinkoff, was the honorary chairman and I was the master of ceremonies. Former associates and residents came from as far away as Japan and Germany and from all over the United States.

After cocktails and a lavish dinner, designated persons gave short speeches exalting Dan's dynamic leadership. Dean Mellinkoff spoke in the name of the medical school faculty and hospital staff. The four hundred people present gave Dan a standing ovation. Dan Morton closed the ceremony by urging the new chairman, Jerry Moore, and his staff to continue the tradition that had been established during the past fifteen years.

30 · The Impact of the Vietnamese War on Academia

FEW people inside or outside America expected that the first cry against the Vietnamese war would come from college and university students. The image of the typical American student was that of a well-behaved young man or woman whose surplus energy was expended harmlessly through attending sport events. Up to the mid-1960s American students had shown little interest in national or international politics and thus were different from Latin American students, who traditionally formed the shock troops of political upheaval and change. I did not think the first wave of protests, marches, and strikes against the war in Berkeley would last, but I was wrong. The Berkeley protests spread to other universities and engaged not only students but also a large part of the faculty, particularly those in philosophy and political science.

Needless to say, I was among those who took an active part in organizing antiwar protests. The generally conservative medical faculty looked on the few of us who opposed the war as radicals—a label that later brought me into direct conflict with the dean of the Medical School and strained our relationship to a point that threatened my position at the university.

I pursued my antiwar activities in many ways. First, I corresponded constantly with senators and congressmen who were opposed to the war, particularly William Fulbright, whose book *The Arrogance of Power* reflected the feelings of many of us about American foreign policy. Also, I was a member of one of the Study Sections of the National Institutes of Health, which met every three months, usually in Washington, to judge applications for federal research grants. So every time I went to Washington, I mixed political activity with my scientific work. Not only did I visit congressmen and senators personally and urge them to support the antiwar protesters, but on occasion I picketed the White House with fellow scientists.

What gave me the most satisfaction in the antiwar movement were my support of the antiwar medical students and my activities as a member of the Committee of Responsibility. American medical students are usually considered benign young men dedicated to their studies who are either apolitical or politically conservative. The UCLA medical students were no exception. Although strikes, marches, and assaults on administration buildings occurred on the main campus, the medical students never participated. One day, however, the Committee of Medical Students Against the War in Vietnam was formed. In a short time they obtained the support of a large number of students, but not of faculty. In fact, the committee was strongly opposed by Dean Mellinkoff and most of the faculty.

The antiwar students petitioned the dean for permission to stand in silent prayer in one of the courtyards of the Medical Center, but permission was denied. The committee then asked me to mediate their dispute with the dean. I confess I was utterly surprised by Mellinkoff's refusal to allow such a peaceful expression of feelings and amazed by his superficial reason, which was that the Medical Center was dedicated to the care of sick people whose condition might be aggravated by the students' "demonstration."

I wrote the dean a polite letter, urging him to modify his stand. I pointed out that the Medical School should consider itself lucky that its students were satisfied simply to stand in silence and pray, and since the gathering would be in the Medical Center courtyard, there was little chance of disturbing patients. Some other professors joined me in defending students' rights. After a lot of negotiation, the medical students were permitted to stand in silent prayer just outside the Medical Center.

My worst clash with the university administration involved my activities with the Committee of Responsibility. This national organization was formed shortly after the escalation of the Vietnamese war, when bombing, defoliation, and napalm took a heavy toll of the South Vietnamese population, particularly children. The main goal of this committee was to furnish medical assistance and rehabilitation to children mutilated by napalm or fragmentation bombs. Many doctors were active on this committee. I myself not only contributed financially, but also devoted a lot of time to raising money and planning the medical-assistance program for the children. After a great effort, and despite incredible obstruction by the State and Defense departments, the committee was able to bring to the United States a number of badly burned and mutilated children. The major problem was finding hospitals for them.

We all felt that the best hospitals were the university facilities on the West Coast. The opportunity to treat children and adults burned with napalm or suffering from bomb fragments under the skin or lodged in the body was unique and would be of tremendous instructional value. However, our repeated attempts to persuade the UCLA administration to admit some of these children to the Medical Center and to accept responsibility for their mutilation were in vain. Everyone, from local administrative officials to Governor Ronald Reagan, raised objections to our involvement in such a politically sensitive program.

The children were finally admitted to various private hospitals in the country, where they were treated and rehabilitated over several years. The Committee of Responsibility defrayed all costs of this project.

A major "fallout" of the Southeast Asian war was in the area of federal support for medical research and scientific training. Both Johnson and Nixon waged an undeclared but very expensive war without increasing taxes to support it. Johnson managed to spend billions of dollars on defense without cutting the NIH budget. When Nixon took over, however, he promised to balance the budget despite huge military expenditures. One of his first acts was to phase out all training programs in the biological sciences. Our program—the first one in the field of reproductive biology, responsible since 1957 for training people from all over the world—was terminated in 1971. I was heartbroken. During the fifteen years of its existence, our program had brought me bright, energetic young people just finished with their residency and had let me make true scientists of them. Our laboratories were labeled "the chairmans' factory" because we supplied so many well-trained people to universities in the United States and abroad. Right up to the last month I received a stream of applications for this program. It was a painful task for me to inform those applicants that we could no longer support their fellowship, because our training program had been terminated.

Fortunately, many eager applicants were able to scrape together savings or borrow money to come work with us for one or two years. Some were also supported by private foundations. Consequently, our training activities have continued with the same intensity up to the present time. We have to be more selective in accepting applicants and confine our program to people who will occupy positions in American universities. Young foreigners may study at their own expense, or with the support of their governments.

Epilogue

MORE than four and a half decades have passed since I left Lebanon on the *Julius Caesar* and about three and a half since I brought Alfredo to Chicago on a DC-3. The world has shrunk in distance considerably during those years. The trips that took one month to Brazil and three days to Chicago now require only a few hours. Man has conquered distance between countries on this planet, and between the planets themselves. Man has driven a motor vehicle on the moon. Satellites and spaceships of every size and shape travel at unimaginable speed, sending pictures of astonishing clarity to television screens on Earth. More and more destructive weapons are devised every day, and "civilized" nations have amassed nuclear bombs sufficient to annihilate every living creature and to obliterate many times over everything that man has created. Our fathers could not have dreamed the fantastic technological advances of the past four decades.

Along with these advances, man has also made great strides in eradicating diseases and improving the health conditions in at least some parts of the world. Malaria, the disease that implanted in me the seed of love for medicine, has been almost totally eradicated. Other diseases, including syphilis, gonorrhea, and tuberculosis, which in the past required years of treatment, can now be cured in a matter of days, or even with one or two injections. The same can be said of most infectious diseases that ravaged entire populations in the past. Moreover, during the last five decades the population of the globe has doubled, from two billion to four billion, and the average life span has increased by more than twenty years. All this has resulted from improved health standards.

Yet one has to ask what moral progress man has made, how much he has advanced in his behavior toward his fellow man. The answer is very little, if any. World War I, with all its horror, destruction, and tragedy, was fought with the hope of all mankind that it would put an end to all wars. Hardly had its damage been repaired when several localized conflicts led to the holocaust of World War II, the devastating effects of which were a thousand times greater. Since the end of that war, not one day has passed without conflict between nations on this earth.

My father's dreams for Lebanon were realized after 1945, when it and other Middle Eastern nations obtained independence. The colonial powers also gave independence to many other nations on the African continent and in the Far East. Independence came, however, more in form than in substance. Instead of food, the great powers gave armaments.

Rachaya was rebuilt after 1925, only to suffer one destruction after another because of the constant conflicts that have gripped the Middle East during the past three decades. Living at the crossroads of Syria, Lebanon, and Israel, the inhabitants of Rachaya and surrounding towns have been caught in indescribable horrors not of

their own making and beyond their control. According
to the latest information, Rachaya is almost totally deserted.

After a short interval of democracy following the collapse of the Vargas regime, Brazil reverted to a military
dictatorship, which has proved just as oppressive as that
of Vargas. São Paulo has grown to be one of the largest,
most polluted, and most congested cities in the world. It
is a city of haphazard skyscrapers. And while the number of moving vehicles has multiplied thousands of
times, the great majority of the city's streets remain as
they were more than fifty years ago. Although many of
its inhabitants take great pride in its growth, many wonder about the future of this metropolis. Nowhere in the
world is the distance between rich and poor so great as
in São Paulo today.

I still work in research and teach at UCLA. Every day
I get as much excitement and joy from an experiment or
a lecture as I did when I started more than three decades
ago. My biggest thrill and pleasure is training postgradu-
ate doctors who come to my laboratories from all over
the world. I am the proudest man on earth every time
one of them leaves to assume a major research or academic position. The NIH still generously supports my
research program. We still live in the same house. Pauline is as active in the community as ever. Robin teaches
philosophy, and Billy attends college.

Looking back on my life, I find little in it that I willed
or planned. As a young shepherd or a latrine-digger in
the prison camp in Lebanon or as a medical student in
Brazil, I never dreamed that one day I would become a
prominent academician and investigator in the United
States of America. Once again I concur with Tolstoy:
"When an apple has ripened and falls, why does it fall?
Because of its attraction to earth, because its stalk with-

ers, because it is dried by the sun, because it grows heavier, because the wind shakes it, or because the boy standing below wants to eat it? Nothing is the cause. All this is only the coincidence of conditions in which all vital organic and elemental events occur."

Index